AF335656

BEYOND THIS LAND OF WHOA

BEYOND THIS LAND OF WHOA

BY CHANDLER W. STERLING

A PILGRIM PRESS BOOK

from United Church Press, Philadelphia

Copyright © 1973 United Church Press
All Rights Reserved

No part of this publication may be reproduced, stored in a retrieval
system, or transmitted in any form or by any means, electronic, me-
chanical, photocopying, recording, or otherwise, without the prior per-
mission of the publisher.

Library of Congress Cataloging in Publication Data

Sterling, Chandler W   Bp., 1911-
  Beyond this land of whoa.
  "A Pilgrim Press book."
  1. Sterling, Chandler W   Bp., 1911-
I. Title.
BX5995.S786A32   283'.092'4 [B]   73-5904
ISBN 0-8298-0261-4

Excerpt on p. 136 is from the hymn "Jesus Calls Us, o'er the Tumult"
by Cecil F. Alexander. The excerpt on p. 140 is from the hymn "There
Is a Blessed Home" by H. W. Baker. For the prayers on pp. 93-94, see
The Book of Common Prayer, 1928, pp. 319-20; for the confirmation
prayer on p. 135, see p. 297.

United Church Press, 1505 Race Street,
Philadelphia, Pennsylvania 19102

To Eleanor I

> *who knew that salvation was available outside the church, but that neither a lady nor a gentleman would avail himself of it . . .*

To Eleanor II

> *who withstood the sopranos in the choir 6-1 . . .*

To Eleanor III

> *who still wonders if this is really the way it all happened . . .*

PREFACE

I PLEAD GUILTY TO RUMMAGING IN THE ATTIC WHILE there is a fire in the basement. Being possessed of a memory which persecutes the past by over-remembering, I reproduce an account of the ways of the child's mind. It is intended for those who will venture into that world at the risk of being frightened by what they might see inside the mind of an Alice who is surrounded by a world full of Red Queens.

Truth and fiction always sleep together, and don't ever allow your Red Queen to persuade you that it is otherwise. Moreover, they always embrace each other in old trunks in attics, and our society is nearly out of both old trunks and attics.

The story is misleading in that the person of Grandma appears to be the subject, certainly to the speed-reader, when it is actually about the lost child who wanders through the rest of his life as an adult still trying to believe that today is real and that everything that happened before was like anything else that happened before breakfast—the last part of the night.

And I don't really think that's so because Grandma did wear a taffeta dress like Virginia did, only hers was blue and whistled when she passed me on her way to the blackboard.

...IN ORDER TO REMEMBER WHEN YOU WERE BORN YOU NEED A GRANDMA....

I WAS BORN AHEAD OF A THUNDERSTORM BECAUSE BEFORE you begin remembering you don't really know whether you were born or not. But I began remembering right before a thunderstorm. I was allowed to sit up late on the front porch because it was too hot upstairs in my room to go to sleep. I was playing with Grandma's mother-of-pearl opera glasses which were fastened on a stick and I aimed them at the street light. Suddenly everything became clear. Not only the street light, but many things could be seen better. Grandma and I sat in the swing which, when I made it go fast like Mrs. Dement did when she came to visit us, would swing back into the woodbine and stir up the mosquitoes. Only tonight we didn't make it go so high because Grandma said it made her dizzy and that when she was in the swing with me please swing slow like a chariot.

While we were sitting there in the dark watching the lightning bugs, Grandma said that it was still and dark on the night that the Lord made the earth, just like tonight only it was further back. I asked Grandma if the earth was created during a thunderstorm and she said she didn't know but probably that came later when Noah had so much trouble, but anyway it was dark when the earth was created and before there was anything there wasn't anything and darkness was on the face of the deep, as the Bible says. When I asked Grandma if God had a deep face she started telling me what happened to me before I could remember anything that happened to me, which has been going on pretty fast ever since I began remembering things.

Before Grandma got started on remembering about me before I remembered, I told her about one of the first things that I did remember and that it had to do with this porch swing and Mrs. Dement last summer. Grandma asked me what that was and I told her about the time that Mrs. Dement came up on the porch for a visit and she sat in the swing as she always did and the faster she swung the faster she talked, or the other way around. She could be heard clear down to Decker's house which is at the other end of the block and facing the cemetery besides. I reminded Grandma that Mrs. Dement was telling her about Mrs. Emerson giving her husband's clothes to Mr. Garnett, the rector of the church, because Mr. Emerson had died beating a horse and where he was going it would be so hot that he wouldn't need any clothes. Mrs. Dement also said that it was a shame, not that Mr. Emerson was going to be hot for a long time, but that he was only five feet three inches tall and had a bay window and that Mr. Garnett was over six feet and looked like a clothes pole and she didn't see how Mr. Garnett could even wear Mr. Emerson's long underwear.

Grandma said, "Great Scott!" (whatever that meant) and Mrs. Dement's feet came down together on the porch floor and the swing stopped and I kept on going and slid right out of the swing and landed on Grandma's darning basket and got the pincushion on my behinder. Then the cat ran in the house because of the noise and the excitement, and Mother ran out of the house and onto the porch to see what had happened and Mrs. Dement started swinging again and talking and Grandma pulled the pincushion off my behinder and I stopped crying and felt better and went in the house with my mother and she gave me a cookie, and Mrs. Dement went on talking.

I went out the back door and started across the vacant lot next to our house to go and see if Freddie could play with me. My behinder still stung a little bit so I laid down on my tummy in the high grass and finished my cookie. Finally I saw an ant come along. He waved his feelers at me as I watched him make his way through the green grass jungle which must have been how it looked to him. I waved back at him and he smiled. He would climb a stalk of grass and then come down again and climb another one. When he would get to the top each time he would look around and wave his feelers at the whole world. It was a long time before any of his friends saw him, but finally one did, and they felt each other all over and stood there and talked to each other for awhile. Then they felt each other again and said goodby and went away in different directions. All the time there was a praying mantis on another green stalk pretending that he was saying his prayers like Mr. Cheadle always looked in church when he was saying his prayers. But the mantis didn't fool me or those ants any more than Mr. Cheadle fooled God. I knew that he was waiting for one of those ants to come close so that he could grab him and have him for lunch. But they never did and the mantis had to wait. And then I was through remembering and stopped talking and Grandma started remembering and she talked awhile.

She said to me, "Jamie, the second day after you were born the doctor said to your father that 'I don't think that the little fellow is going to live.' That was you. Then the doctor told your father that maybe he had better go ahead and get you baptized. Your father said that he didn't know what difference a few drops of water would make, and I told your father that a few drops of ink on a check make a big difference, and he didn't have anything to say to that."

Grandma went on to explain that she had sent away to the Holy Land for a bottle of water from the Jordan River, and the family (meaning my mother and Grandma specially) was going to make a big thing over the baptism of the first born, who was me. I was taken out of the hospital and carried down to the church where Mr. Garnett baptized me and the Jordan River was spilled all down the front of my baptismal dress which had lace on it and it all turned brown.

She told me that Uncle Charlie from Chicago and Uncle Ernest from Gap Grove were my godfathers and that Mrs. Kent was my godmother, only Mrs. Kent was the only godparent who came to the baptism because Uncle Charlie was busy selling insurance and Uncle Ernest was not only snowed in on the farm but was milking the cows at the same time.

When Mrs. Kent went home she took a piece of pink cardboard and with her scissors she cut out a little lamb and wrote "Jamie" on it and fastened a blue ribbon to it. Then next Sunday when she came to church, Mrs. Kent pinned the lamb with my name on it to a large poster which at the top had a picture of a curly-haired baby clutching a rattle and smiling at everybody. I was told that the gold lettering at the top of the poster explained that we were all "Little Helpers." There were other lambs up on the board too. There were blue lambs for Freddie and Gerald and Todd and there were pink lambs for Virginia and Evelyn. And that was about it for the lambs.

Grandma said that my father took me back to the hospital to live out my days, and five years later I am still at it, but I didn't stay in the hospital that long but just for about two weeks and then I was brought home where I cried for two years when something was wrong, which was most of the time. My father said, "Isn't that kid ever going to get over the shock of being born?" And I guess maybe I never did. But I don't remember anything about that except for what Grandma told me before I went up to bed before the thunderstorm.

When we got upstairs, Grandma read me a story about a king who didn't have any clothes on but he thought he did and the picture showed him all dressed and going down the street like he was hurrying late to church. I knew that wasn't the way the story said, but Grandma told me that they had to put clothes on him in a picture even if he didn't have any on in the story. I thought that was a dumb story, and a dumb picture too.

I went to sleep. Then I woke up. It was raining in my window. The window shade was flapping and banging because it wanted to get away and hide in the closet where the wind couldn't find it. The thunder was awful loud and shook the whole house and sounded like when coal was shoveled down the long chute into the cellar, only louder. The lightning was so bright and near that it crackled like the world's biggest bonfire and the rain hissed against the broad leaves of the maple trees, and I was afraid. I remembered Grandma's story about God creating the world in darkness and I thought maybe he was doing the world over tonight and I was right in the middle of it. So I called out to Grandma. She would know what to do.

I heard her fumbling down the long hall in the dark. She bumped into the bathroom door and said, "Great Scott!" For a moment, in the yellow flash of lightning shadow, I saw her standing there holding on to her nose and weaving a little bit as she recovered from the collision. Grandma went into the bathroom and closed the door. She came back out right away as if she remembered that I was the one who called to her. She came into my room and turned on the light, only it didn't go on because something happened down at the dam. So she went away again to get a lamp but she bumped her head on my door this time, which had blown halfway shut, and she said, "Great Scott" again and finally came back with a lighted kerosene lamp and put it in the wall bracket alongside the dresser.

Her long white braids swayed back and forth, making flickering shadows slide up and down the wall on the other side of the room. Her big, bunioned feet padded about as she opened doors and closed windows. Her flanneled figure approached me and she got into my bed and held me close to her front and she told me not to be afraid. And I wasn't because I knew that God would take the storm away and do his creating somewhere else, now that Grandma was here. I also knew that the bad fairy wouldn't dare try to get me while Grandma was around. And she didn't.

Grandma told me the story of when she was a little girl on a farm on the great plains. She said that once upon a time there wasn't any thing or any person out there at all and that even God didn't like it that way. So he got to creating again. He made it rain hard and started rivers and lakes. Then he made the grass grow. It grew so fast and so high that he had to do something else. So he made the buffalo come up out of the ground in order to keep the grass down. But the grass was so good that there were more and more buffalo and pretty soon the earth was so thick with buffalo that you couldn't see the grass, so God had another problem. Next he created the Indian and he told him to take care of the buffalo and in return the Indian could have all the buffalo that he needed for meat and clothing and blankets and everything. And so God did.

Then one day a white man came along and the Indian asked him to go hunting with him. And after awhile more white men came and hunted more buffalo, and then the white man started to hunt the Indian too. The buffalo became angry and they all disappeared back into the ground and said that they wouldn't come out again until the white man left the country because the Indian should not have let the white man hunt with him in the first place. I thought that over for a while and then asked Grandma if that was why she moved back to Illinois. She said, "No, but I had to come back and meet Grandpa." I could hear him snoring the covers off his bed in the other room. And I thought some more about the Indians and the buffalo.

Grandma began to sing very softly. She sang her favorite hymn, "There is a blessed home, beyond this land of whoa; where trials never come, nor tears or sorrow flow. Wait but a little while in uncomplaining love. His own most gracious smile, shall welcome you above."

I thought, "Yes, this is the Land of Whoa, where nobody can do what he wants to do without somebody telling you not to." Then I went back to sleep.

...TONSILS, SALT MACKEREL, AND MRS. EELLS, WHO WAS A HUNDRED AND FOUR...

IN THE MORNING A WOODPECKER WOKE ME UP. HE WAS trying to peck worms out of the tin roof over my bedroom and I think that his bill was getting flat because he flew away to find a stone where he could sharpen it up again. My mother came into my room about the time that the factory whistle blew from the Roper Piano Plant. She helped me get dressed after she had washed me off because in all the excitement of last night the bed was wet, and me too, and not from the rain. Then she said that we would not have time to eat breakfast but that we would go right to the hospital instead. I thought that something had happened to my father, but I could hear him snoring the covers off, so I knew he wasn't sick. I didn't say goodby to Grandma or Grandpa, but I peeked into their room to see if he had a prayer book under his chin. That's what was done with Great-grandma after she fell down the back stairs and the Lord called her home and Mr. Staples, the undertaker, hadn't come to our house yet. Besides, Grandpa had his elevens up which Grandma explained meant that he was so old that his neck was getting tired of holding up his head and one of these days he would fall over and the Lord and Mr. Staples would come and get him too. But Grandpa was sleeping

on top of the covers and had his feet crossed which
Grandpa always said that he had a right to do ever
since he had been a pilgrim to Jerusalem, where he had
never really been but thought he had because he had
read Hurlbut's *Illustrated Bible Stories* so much.

Well anyway, the hospital was only three blocks from
home so my mother and I walked over because only my
father knew how to drive the Ford anyway. I saw that
woodpecker sharpening his bill on Charlie McCorry's
cement bird bath. He was talking to two robins who were
having a noisy bath and throwing water all around. Then
Freddie's dog, Beezer, smiled at me from the front porch
where he was guarding Miss Pomeroy's parrot who was
getting his morning air and whistling at my mother. I
wanted to go down the alley and across Leake's backyard because it was shorter but my mother made me stay
on the sidewalk, which I did, most of the way, except
twice.

When we came to the hospital a lady met us at the door
and she was dressed all in white like the girl behind the
fountain at Finalli's Ice Cream Parlor, only the hospital
lady had a big front on her that made her look like she
had a pillow stuck in her dress. She took me by the hand
and walked with me into a room that had a bed in it, so
I told the white woman that I just got up. She didn't
explain anything but turned to my mother and told her
to go sit in the waiting room. And she did, and the pillow
lady took all my clothes off me and laid them on a chair
and put a night gown on me that tied in the back. It
scratched too. She asked me if I would like a ride on
the elevator because they had one there like the one
down at the Bee Hive Department Store. It looked like a

great big birdcage and a man who looked like an owl
made it go up and down. When we got to the top of the
building the man stopped the elevator and smoothed out
his feathers and turned his head fast and stared at me,
but I marched right past him and we went into a room
that was white, like the Purity Bakery on Galena Avenue
near the bridge. I went over to a big window and looked
out over the river and the dam where all the electricity
got stuck last night and made the lights go out. I could
see the Cement Plant switch engine down on the tracks
below but I couldn't hear it, but I could see Cassius
McClanahan's elbow. He was the engineer.

I heard some people come into the room and I turned
around to see who they were. I saw a lot of people all
dressed in white. They had on white masks and only their
eyes showed. I didn't know any of them, but they knew
me because they said, "Good morning, Jamie." I didn't
feel like saying anything because I was beginning not
to want to be there any more. I watched the man who
was putting on brown rubber gloves and snapping them
at everybody and wiggling his fingers like a spider
warming up to grab a fly. I ran toward the door because
I was scared, but a big man in white grabbed me and
lifted me up onto a high, hard table and held me down.
The big woman with the pillow front pressed a rag over
my nose that was filled with awful smelly stuff that made
me gag. My head began to go around and there were loud
noises like thunder and lightning and switch engines and
woodpeckers on tin roofs. I cried out to Grandma to
come and get me, but I was in the Land of Whoa where
tears and sorrows flow and I didn't remember anything
until I woke up with an awful sore throat and the inside

of my nose was sharp. Then I remembered, and what I remembered was bad.

The people in the white gowns, the white masks, and the brown squiggly rubber gloves had all gone away. I was under the back porch alone. I watched a freight train chuff around the edge of the cistern lid and crawl up the wall because it had a thousand legs instead of wheels. The engineer was a praying mantis with an engineer's cap on his head. He waved his feelers at me and made the train chase the ants which were running here and there on the wall. Then I saw Mrs. Dement holding her eyeballs in her hands and pulling pins and needles out of them and throwing them at the cat, swinging and talking all the time.

Then I was back in bed in a white room and wasn't under the back porch any more. The pillow lady was cleaning me up because I had been sick. She talked quietly and said that everything was going to be all right. I wondered how she knew that because she didn't see everything that was going on under the back porch a minute ago.

Late in the afternoon I woke up. I didn't hurt so bad now but I wasn't feeling too good either. I wasn't sick any more, but still nobody came around. Not even Grandma. At last my father came to see me and we had some ice cream together and I began to feel better. He promised to take me fishing next week and I told him that Grandma was going to take me fishing when we took the boat ride on the Guild Picnic next week. My father said, "Oh," and then we didn't talk much and he didn't say if he knew what happened to me upstairs or not. So we just ate the ice cream.

Another lady in white came in the room. She had a flat front and was tall and skinny. But she was nice to me and put my clothes on me and said that I had been a good boy and now my father could carry me home. I guess she didn't know what happened upstairs either. When we got home my mother put me back in bed and then she went away without saying anything. After awhile Grandma came in my room and she got me up and took me in her arms and we sat down in the rocking chair. She cried a little bit. And I cried a little bit too. Then she held me against her front and she sang softly, "There is a blessed home beyond this Land of Whoa." I hoped so. Her tears fell on my cheek again and I felt warm and good all over. When I was in her arms I forgot all my hurt and my scare and I left the Land of Whoa because I went back to sleep.

It wasn't very long after my operation that my Grandma told me that I was invited to go on the picnic that St. Ann's Guild went on every year. Everybody took the boat ride on Mr. Espy's new gasoline launch because he was a carpenter and built the boat and Mr. Espy said he could start the engine by using carpenter's cuss words on the motor and then the flywheel would spin. Well, I got to go and it was on a Thursday and Mr. Garnett, the rector, got to go too, along with me and all the grand-mothers. There were some spinster ladies too, like Miss Scanlon, Juliana Pankhurst, and Nellie Eustace who had a mustache. And the Misses Eells, of whom there were three. All deaf. But I got to go and I decided that I would go fishing. I went down in the cellar of our house and I found an old umbrella that had blown inside out. I tore off all the umbrella stuff and I had a fishing rod. I got some string off the grocery package that had the sack that held rice, which I don't like. Then I took a safety pin for a hook so that I wouldn't hurt the fish when I caught him. And I cut a piece of a Parker House roll for bait and I was ready to go fishing.

Grandma and I walked down to the dock from our house. We had to go through Bluff Park, then go down a wood bridge and a steep path and go by Sam Watson's lower ice house and Ned Howell's skate-sharpening place and we were there and Mr. Espy was waiting for us. He told me that he smoked sawdust in his pipe because he could make his own tobacco but I think he was fooling me, but maybe he wasn't. Anyway, we all got aboard and Mr. Espy started turning the flywheel on the motor, only he didn't cuss because the ladies of St. Ann's Guild would be shocked, especially Miss Scanlon and the Misses Eells, who couldn't hear anything anyway but they came along for the ride.

Mr. Espy finally got the motor going. He was so tired from all that that he just sat down and puffed. Then he lit his pipe and then he untied the boat which by that time had almost pulled the dock out into the river, but Mr. Garnett wasn't there yet. Pretty soon we could see him pedaling along on his bicycle from clear down by the wire screen factory. He put his bicycle up in the crotch of the tree and he came on the boat and somebody asked him to say a prayer. Which he did. And he prayed that nobody would drown in the deep. I wondered in the deep what, but I didn't say anything but he went on praying and he prayed for a rattlesnake to bite Mr. Thomson because a small rattlesnake had bitten his son and he had recovered because he became a good man afterwards, and was on the vestry. Now Mr. Garnett wanted the Lord to send a bigger rattlesnake to bite his father and make a better man out of him. I wondered if he would get on the vestry, too. And then we started up the river.

I put my line in the water and waited. And waited. Nothing happened so I gave the pole to Grandma and let her fish and I went up front to talk to Mr. Espy and watch the flywheel go around which was throwing oil drops on the Misses Eells only they were watching the water and didn't know about the oil drops until they got home. Finally, Mr. Espy told me that he thought something was going on with Grandma, so I went back to the end of the boat. She had caught a fish on my line! I pulled him in and he was already very dead and sort of tired. And I felt pretty good but I didn't want to catch any more fish because the next day I had to eat him and I asked Grandma why he tasted so salty and she said, "It was that kind of a fish," and besides she said it was a mackerel, which Mr. Espy said was an Irish fish that was only caught on Fridays. He and Grandma laughed because Mr. Espy lived right across the street and the next day wanted to know how I liked the fish. So I didn't go fishing any more but I think they were fooling me and the Misses Eells didn't think it was very funny either.

But about three days later, after I had been playing in the vacant lot with Freddie and Virginia and Franklin and Todd, my grandma told me that she and I were going to make a call and that we were going to Mrs. Eells's house where the Misses Eells lived. Mrs. Eells was full of wrinkles and she wasn't much bigger than I. I asked

Grandma how old she was and Grandma said that Mrs. Eells was almost as old as God and my father laughed and said that she must have helped with the dishes at the Last Supper and Grandma didn't think that was so funny and I guess I didn't either. But, anyway, we went to the Eells's house and it was a long walk. We had to go down four blocks past the church where Mr. Garnett prayed, and then under the Illinois Central Railroad tracks. I saw Cassius McClanahan's elbow again but he didn't see me, and then we got to the Eells's house.

Grandma and I went up to the door on the outside and rang the bell and nothing happened. We waited and I got to ring the bell again. And nothing happened again. I got to ring it four more times and nothing happened and Grandma said that maybe we had better try the back door. When Grandma knocked on the back door it opened all by itself and the cat walked out. Then we went into the kitchen and Grandma "yoo-hooed" and Mrs. Eells said, "Is that you, Nellie?" And Grandma said, "yes," and tried to find Mrs. Eells who, at the age of a hundred and four, was on the floor in the pantry because she fell off the stepladder while putting shelf paper up high because her daughters couldn't climb ladders. Mrs. Eells couldn't move so she and Grandma talked for awhile and then we went in the other room and there were the Misses Eells waiting for the doorbell to ring only they were depending on Mrs. Eells to answer the door on account of they couldn't hear the bell ring anyway.

Grandma had to do a lot of yelling to get them to follow her out into the kitchen, which Grandma did, and the Misses Eells did and then everybody started running around and crying. Grandma went next door and got the neighbors to get the doctor. By the time he got there, Grandma had to go back to the neighbors and call Mr. Staples, the undertaker, and Mr. Garnett, the rector. They both showed up about the same time. Mr. Garnett prayed and Mr. Staples brought in a long basket and together they put Mrs. Eells in the basket and went out the back door and everybody started crying again. Then Mr. Garnett came back and started praying over the Misses Eells, and they didn't hear a word he said, even though I thought it was pretty loud. Then I let the cat back in the house and Grandma and I went home and now I guess Grandma is the oldest lady in town, except, of course, for the Misses Eells, who won't last long now because there isn't anybody around the house who can answer the doorbell and put shelf paper in the pantry.

...FALLING PIANOS, FLUSHINGS, AND STAINED GLASS, MOSTLY...

It was about this time that Grandma thought that I was getting to be a big boy and so one day she said, "Jamie, you are getting to be a big boy. Do you think that you are big enough to take Grandpa down to the City Hall?" I already knew that Grandpa had a stroke. Grandma told me all about it and that's why the elevens were up and the prayer book was always alongside the bed. Sometimes Grandpa could not find his way downtown. He would forget where he was going and what he was doing. Once he thought he was in Peoria and that the City Hall had been moved and nobody told him about it. Then he would start calling for Edna but nobody could ever find out who Edna was because Grandpa couldn't remember either, but my father laughed and laughed and nobody thought it was funny but him.

The reason that Grandpa went to the City Hall every day was because he was the city treasurer. Grandma said that as long as Grandpa had a pen in his hand and a ledger in front of him then he knew what to do and didn't make mistakes like my father's bookkeeper did. So I started walking to the City Hall with Grandpa. I learned how to button his shoes and help him put on his alpaca coat after Grandma got his baggy trousers on him. I would bring him his gold watch with the gold chain and the Elk's tooth on it and Grandpa used to tell me to be careful that the tooth didn't bite me but it never did.

One time when Grandpa was mixed up and thought he was in Peoria, I walked him past the Roper Piano Plant because sometimes they lowered pianos out of the attic on ropes. One day they did and the rope broke. The piano dropped three floors and went through the platform and nearly squashed Mr. Cropsey who was helping. The noise was like musical thunder and kept on going awhile after the piano hit the platform and went through to the ground. We went by there many times on our way to the City Hall but I never saw another piano fall.

One day when Grandpa and I were going by the Roper Piano Plant and looking for pianos to be lowered down the outside and maybe to fall, he started mumbling something about William Jennings Bryan. I said, "Mr. Bryan doesn't live here. We are out in front of Mr. Cropsey's house." Grandpa said that he was in Peoria. But Mr. Cropsey wasn't in Peoria. He came running right then around the outside of the house and Mrs. Cropsey was close behind him with a hoe. Grandpa said, "Good morning, Edna," to Mr. Cropsey. But Mr. Cropsey kept on going, and so did Grandpa and I until we came to the City Hall and Mr. Cropsey went the other way and Mrs. Cropsey went out in the garden and did the hoeing herself and then probably went in and did the dishes. I must remember to tell Grandma all about this because maybe she knows what the trouble is with Grandpa not remembering. Except he always remembers how to keep books. Mayor Palmer says so and he ought to know being the mayor and everything and knowing where he is all the time. He even tells the policeman what to do because once he told Mr. Fansteel to lock me up and Mr. Fansteel was going to do it, only the mayor was fooling. Everybody besides the mayor says that Grandpa is a good treasurer—for an old codger. I think so myself. Sometimes Grandpa calls me a young codger, unless he thinks he is in Peoria. When he calls me a young codger I laugh and feel good until I remember that his elevens are up and he can't see them because they are on the back of his neck. But I can, and they stand up real sharp sometimes and I think maybe I had better go and get the prayer book for his chin. But Grandma says, "Not yet. The Lord isn't ready to call him home." And I guess maybe Mr. Staples isn't ready either, and they have to be ready at the same time.

One day after I had taken Grandpa to the City Hall, the mayor asked him if he was going to do the books today or was he going to Peoria. And Grandpa said, "No, Edna is in Jerusalem." And they both laughed, because Grandpa knew that sometimes he didn't know. Then I went across the street to my father's store, but I had to wait for Mr. Dauntler's dray horses and wagon to go past first.

My other grandpa was sitting on the stool behind the cigar counter and talking to Mr. Cole who held up his big mustache as he aimed at the spittoon. I got up on Grandpa Too's lap but he was smoking a big cigar and the smoke hurt my eyes. So I got down and went to the back of the store to see my father, but he was mixing smelly medicine, so I thought I would go to the bathroom.

The bathroom was down in the black cellar where the floor was covered with cinders and there were rats and mice too. The walls were lined with dusty shelves and there were all kinds of boxes and bottles there. The boxes had printing on them that told what was on the inside. When I went downstairs Carl was already there getting some turpentine out of a big barrel and he dribbled it all over his shoes and said, "Oh, hell." And then he saw me and said, "Hello, Son." After I said hello to Carl, I asked him what was in the big boxes and packages. He said that they were counter and show-window displays that were saved to use again next year. One of the displays was a picture of a hobo chopping a block of ice with an axe. I asked Carl what the words said underneath and Carl said, "How to Break up a Cold—Use a Bromo-Quinine." I thought it was a dumb sign because who would break ice with an axe anyway, especially if you had a cold and weren't supposed to be outdoors anyway.

Then Carl went upstairs with the turpentine and I went to the bathroom only there wasn't any tub or wash basin. And besides I had to step up on a platform and open the door to get in and there it was. It had a pipe going up the wall to a big box which had a chain coming out of it and a knob handle at the other end of the chain. When the chain was pulled, the water came roaring down into the bowl and sounded like a waterfall. I guess so, because I never really heard one. Carl said that the box was full of used beer. I wonder how he got up there to fill it up, but I never asked him because I thought he would laugh and then I would know that he was fooling me again.

While I was in the bathroom I could hear people walking around on the floor upstairs. As soon as I was finished, I pulled the chain and the lights went out and the door slammed down onto the floor. I yelled and hollered but nobody heard me. This got all the rats curious and they came out and started knocking bottles over. The bottles would go "klunk" on the cinder floor and stuff would run out of the broken bottles. Carl told me it happened all the time.

Even if nobody heard me, Carl came back down and found me scared and crying a little. Then Carl said, "I tell you what we'll do. We'll shoot rats!" He went down to the other end of the cellar and got a twenty-two rifle. I sat down beside him on a box. Then Carl would toss a piece of coal against the stone wall and we would sit there real quiet and wait.

Pretty soon a rat would stick his head out to see what was going on and then Carl would shoot him. He did a flip in the air and fell on the cinders dead. Then another rat would come to see what had happened and Carl would shoot him and pretty soon we had several rats, except for one that saw Carl first and ducked.

I got to hold the gun while Carl gathered up all the rats and carried them upstairs and out into the alley behind the store. Then he cut their tails off and put them in a paper bag and gave them to me and put the rest of the rats in the garbage can. Carl told me to take the rat tails over to the City Hall where Grandpa worked and they would give me two cents for each tail, which the mayor did, telling me that I was a fine fellow because he was glad to see that I was helping the city get rid of rats. I got twelve cents for six rat tails. I spent the money for candy which I was going to give Virginia for Christmas, but Freddie and me ate most of it first and didn't feel so good afterwards.

Getting back to the bathroom. After that experience I was afraid to flush the toilet anymore anywhere because I was afraid that the lights might go out and it would be dark and maybe a door would slam shut somewhere and then what would I do if nobody heard me for a long time like down in the church basement when everybody was upstairs listening to Mr. Garnett. So I didn't flush toilets anymore. Then I would get scolded. I had lots of trouble at home about this, but I couldn't help it. It made even more trouble just before Christmas.

It was the front stairway at our house that started everything. When I went up the stairway I had to pass two stained-glass windows. There was one on each landing. The window on the lower landing had a big orange flower with long petals that looked like squiggly spider legs. The window at the top of the stairs was a Tiffany window. Grandma said it was. My father said that it was the last window that Mr. Tiffany ever did and that when his wife saw it she gave Mr. Tiffany a piece of rope and told him to go out to the barn and hang himself. I thought the window was real pretty unless you looked at it for a long time. It was the picture of a woman wearing a nightgown and she had wings and a horn in her hand which she was getting ready to blow. Her hair was gold, green, or brown, depending upon what the weather was outside and how bright or how cloudy it was. She always watched me come up the stairs and she looked at me as if she knew I had been bad again and I could never remember what I had done. The big wings that she wore looked more like fish scales with hair on them. I didn't like them.

There was a cement factory near town where they

made cement out of rock. My father told me that men pounded the big rocks into dust and put it in sacks and took it somewhere else and took it out of the sacks and poured water on it and mixed sand in it and made sidewalks out of it when it got hard again, and sometimes streets and curbs. He said that the rocks were so big to start with that men used extra big firecrackers called dynamite which smashed it up into smaller pieces. It made the whole world shake when they did that, only you couldn't hear it, but just feel it, except sometimes you could hear it if it was quiet and Mrs. Dement wasn't talking on the front porch.

This day that I am talking about you couldn't hear but you could feel it because the door was closed because it was winter. I had gone to the bathroom and didn't flush the toilet. When I started down the stairs the house shook. I looked at the window that had the woman on it with the feather scales. She moved. Her mouth cracked open and she grinned at me, and her mouth bent down as though she was angry and was going to bite me because I hadn't flushed.

I ran fast down the stairs past her and this time God shook the house. When I got to the lower landing I saw the orange flower turn into a spider and it tried to grab me as I went by. Then I fell down on the landing in front of the squiggly window and the window reached out toward me and broke and it tried to spider me and it clawed me and I cried for Grandma and pushed his claws off me and cut my hands and there was blood on them and I was afraid of everything, God too, and I looked around for Mr. Staples the undertaker, but he wasn't there.

My mother came into the hallway and saw me there on the floor bloody and crying and waiting for Mr. Staples. She said, "Well, I never!" My mother called Grandma but she didn't hear me because Mrs. Dement was in the kitchen and talking. Then my mother said, "March right back upstairs and flush that toilet." I had to go back up those stairs because my mother made me do it. So I did, and the spider didn't get me, but the woman in the window watched me with those stary eyes and that crooked, mean mouth and I could tell that she was angry with me too.

I was afraid to go into the bathroom because God might start shaking the house again and then maybe it would get dark and doors would slam. There was another stained-glass window in the bathroom, but I could see that nothing had happened to that one, but it was plain anyway. But something might happen to it. Especially if I flushed the toilet. So I didn't, but just stood around the hallway for awhile hoping that my mother wouldn't hear it if I didn't because of Mrs. Dement's jawing.

Only I came down the back stairs where there weren't any windows, just unopened Christmas presents on the steps, and the ironing board. I went out to the kitchen and my mother washed off the blood from my hands which had dried by now and which I don't think she saw before. She said that I was naughty because I didn't do what she told me to do. She said to march right back up the front stairs and flush the toilet this time or I would get a hard spanking. I could not do what my mother told me to do and I started to cry. Then she told me that if I didn't march right up those stairs and flush that toilet then not only could I not be a shepherd in the Christmas pageant but I would not get any Christmas presents either. I was in a fix because she said that she had already written Santa Claus and told him that I didn't deserve any Christmas presents because I never flushed the toilet.

I ran away from her and hid under the grand piano and scared the cat. But I didn't cry any more. I just thought about things for a long time and why I couldn't do what my mother asked me to do. Then I waited for God to shake the house again. But he didn't and I began to feel better. I guess God was busy doing something else and didn't notice me.

When my father came home for supper my mother told him that I had been naughty and she told him to take me upstairs and spank me. So my father took me upstairs. He didn't say anything but walked into my room and sat on the edge of the bed and grabbed my shoulders and gave me a hard shaking. He didn't understand what it was all about, and I couldn't explain to him why I couldn't do what my mother told me to do. But he didn't shake me very hard or very long, but when he got through he had three faces, and I felt funny and sick. Two of his faces were fuzzy and one was sad. He left me and I sat on my bed and looked out the window.

There was that woodpecker with the dull bill out there on a tree limb and his mother was with him. I watched him peck away until he found a worm, which he did, and it was a brown, squiggly one. And his mother came over and took it away from him and ate it herself. Then he pecked away some more. Every time he would find a worm his mother would come and take it away from him and he didn't get anything to eat.

At last he flew away and she flew after him and then there wasn't anybody left until a robin came up on the limb. He was all fluffed up and mad about something. I think he had just had a fight with his mother and finally got away from her.

So it was a long time before I could tell my mother that I was sorry, because I wasn't and I couldn't tell her why. When Christmas was only three days away and I still had the pain in my tummy I went to her and said that I was sorry, but I kept my fingers and my legs crossed when I said so because I wasn't really sorry. I lied because I didn't want to miss Christmas. And because I lied I had a good Christmas and my mother never knew the difference and I got to be a shepherd in the Christmas pageant. Anyway, I didn't have to flush the toilet and that was a good thing because I couldn't make myself do it anyway.

The day before Christmas I went to the toilet again and my mother did not hear me not flush the toilet. Then I went to my bedroom window and looked out and there was that woodpecker again. Only his mother wasn't with him this time and he had all the worms he wanted for himself. Then he flew down to the kitchen window and got himself some bread crumbs that Grandma had put outside. She always said, "To the hungry man and the winter birds no crust is hard." And I guess it isn't, even if it is, if you get what I mean. Then he flew by my window again and he smiled at me and he waved a wing. He made me feel better about everything because now I know that even birds have trouble with their mothers sometimes.

...ANCESTORS, INSECTS, PORCH ROOFS, POLICE, AND THE LADY GHOST...

MY FATHER SAID THAT MY MOTHER AND I WERE GOING TO visit Grandpa and Grandma Passmore next Sunday after church and that we would be over there in time for dinner. Grandpa Too and Grandma Too lived across the river on the far side of town. They had a small house and a big barn and two sheds because they were retired farmers. They had a big garden too. And some apple and cherry trees and a flower garden and a grape arbor. Grandma Kingsley, who lived with me, and liked to sing hymns to "knit the raveled sleeve of care," as she said, and also took care of me mostly, told me that she was a Stephens and although the Passmores had been around the country for three generations and were related to the Lawrences they were still dirt farmers at heart like the Schirmers but at least they didn't keep pigs or guinea hens.

But I was glad to go to Grandpa and Grandma Passmore's house because of the interesting smells and things to look at in the barn, the two sheds and the closed-off spare room. This room was my favorite place because it had an Edison Gramophone with a big horn shaped like a morning glory flower and painted purple and gold. It still worked. When I went up to that room I would put an old disc record on and crank up the machine with a crank and listen to "Cohen on the Telephone." It always came out the same way and Mr. Cohen never could make central understand that the storm window had blown off the house.

There was a big bed in that room and Grandma Too had all her blankets and quilts and comforters spread out on top so that they didn't have to be folded, so they weren't because Grandma Too said that to fold them made them weak. Maybe it did. They smelled of moth balls. I found some between each blanket and quilt. There were old trunks up there too, and they were filled with letters and old newspapers and pictures of people who looked as if they were trying to keep their false teeth from slipping out. The women wore long dresses and high collars that choked them and maybe that's why their faces were tight and puffy. The men weren't that way but they had long whiskers and I couldn't really tell, except they all looked as sad as if the dog had died. But maybe they were just sad when they thought about how grim and uncomfortable the women were.

Downstairs in the parlor there was a big Bible on the table and alongside it was a picture of God in a rainstorm and his beard was blowing in the wind and he looked all wet and he was angry about something and pointing to some Roman numerals on a stone slab. He sure was mad at somebody and I'm glad it wasn't me on that day when he had his picture taken. I bet he even scared the man that took the picture.

On the front page of the Bible there were a lot of names written down. I asked Grandpa Too who those people were. Then he read the list to me.

"Now look, Jamie," he started, "here at the top of the

page it reads: 'James Richey Passmore, b. Lyme, Connecticut, 1755. d. Braintrim County, Pennsylvania, 1828.' It says here that he was hit by a falling tree. I guess he was on the wrong side when it was chopped down." Grandpa bent over and used the spittoon. After he wiped his chin he started telling me some more about him.

"He was your great-great-grandfather, Jamie. He was a Tory and he wouldn't fight in George Washington's army because he had a job working for the king of England and the king was paying his salary and bought him a place to live." I thought that was the right thing to do, but I was interrupting Grandpa Too and he said so, and then he went on explaining. "He was run out of town by the men who had joined up in Washington's army and he went up in the mountains in Pennsylvania where he died at the age of seventy-three." I thought that was very old and no wonder he got squashed by a tree because he probably couldn't see it coming and maybe couldn't get out of the way in time in case he did see it because he probably had rheumatism, like most old people. Grandpa went on to say that Pennsylvania was where my great-grandfather was born, and he showed it to me in the book: "James Richey Passmore, b. Braintrim County, Pennsylvania, 1810. d. Davis County, Illinois, 1858 when he fell through the ice on Rock River as he was driving a herd of cows over to the Lawrence farm in the dead of winter." He caught pneumonia and galloping consumption, and I should think he would have.

I asked Grandpa if he was a Tory, too, and he said that it didn't matter any more because all that mattered now was being a Republican. I told Grandpa that the only kind of Tory that I ever heard about was a Supposit Tory. And he laughed and leaned over the spittoon again and wiped his chin and said that he bet that Grandpa Passmore was a pain in the butt to General Washington. And I'll bet he was too. George Washington chopped down a tree once, but he was younger then and he got out of the way in time and got to be President which is a good thing because he was a Republican.

Then Grandpa Too showed me his name, and he was James Richey Passmore the third and he was born in 1846. Grandpa Too said he was a warm member and I thought so too but I wasn't sure whether he meant that he had heat for his rheumatism. I don't know. Then Grandpa said that he wasn't dead yet. Anybody could tell that. He showed me my father's name and he was James Richey Passmore the fourth and he was born on the farm in 1884. Down at the bottom of the page was my name, James Richey Passmore V, because I guess they ran out of letters and got down to numeral letters. Grandpa Too told me all this and then he spit in the spittoon again and wiped his chin and his whiskers this time which had brown stain on them where he hadn't been too neat.

I got to stay overnight at Grandma and Grandpa Passmore's house on account of Grandpa Kingsley was about to have another stroke. It all turned out that he didn't. He just got to thinking that he was in Peoria with Edna, only he wasn't.

The next day being Monday, Grandma Too could work. But not on Sunday because that was the Lord's Day as everybody knows. Bright and early in the morning, after I ate my cornflakes and had to eat some corn meal mush, I went out into the vegetable garden to help

Grandma Too take the bugs off the potato plants. She showed me how to hold a pie tin with kerosene in it in my left hand and take a paring knife in my right hand and push the bugs off the leaves into the kerosene. When she started me doing this she went in the house to do the dishes and I stayed and knocked off potato bugs for awhile. I must have knocked a million of them into the pie tin with the kerosene and they were having a dreadful time of it. The more I knocked off the more there seemed to be. They oozed out of the plant I think. So I got tired of doing that and I went into the shed and looked around, which was much more interesting.

There were some old tools there and I didn't even know what they were for. There were some old harnesses and some hames, which are horse collars. And boxes and wasps and yellowjackets. And their nests, along with the hornets, were all over the place. They would bob and dance about in the air and buzz around the ceiling and bump their heads. Then they would get mad and complain about it all to their friends who were doing the same thing. But they never bothered me so I let them be.

Pretty soon I could smell something cooking so I went into the kitchen and the dinner was on the woodstove cooking and the cat was there too, smelling the dinner, which was catfish. There was a pump on the sink and the cat was sitting alongside that while watching the catfish get cooked. On the shelf over the sink there was a tall drinking glass only it didn't have any water in it but instead had pieces of paper folded longways. Grandma said that they were tapers. She used them to start a bigger fire in the stove from an old coal. Sometimes she would stick the paper in the stove and light the paper, then use the taper to light a lamp. But that was always when it was getting dark, and that way Grandma didn't have to use many matches. And she didn't. "Waste not, want not," she said.

When I left food on my plate she would say, "Waste not, want not." And I didn't want any more, and with the cat around nothing would be wasted, so I didn't know what she was talking about and I think maybe sometimes she didn't either. Every time that she would say one of her sayings Grandpa Too would say, "Now, Dorrie, he's just a little boy." But she went right ahead anyway and reminded me, when I couldn't find my hat that "There's a place for everything and everything in its place." I guess so. But that went on all the time at Grandpa and Grandma Passmore's.

In the afternoon I went back home alone because I was big enough to find my way across the bridge and up the hill and past the City Hall. But I didn't stop there because I knew that Grandpa was home, and all the time he was thinking that he was in Peoria with Edna. Or maybe Jerusalem this time. Anyway, I bet his elevens were up. But Grandpa was fine and was winding up the phonograph with his good hand and was getting ready to play the "Battle Hymn of the Republic" again. He played it over and over and we all pretended that we liked it because it made Grandpa quiet and he didn't keep calling for Edna and sometimes he came back fast from Peoria when he heard the silver cornet play the chorus. Then he would try to march around the room only he stumbled unless I marched with him. About dinner time, Grandpa was put to bed by Grandma and we all had supper. I peeked in the room to see if the prayer book was under his chin and the pennies on his eyelids. But they weren't yet, and Mr. Staples didn't come, so I guess God was too busy to come and get Grandpa. So I went outdoors after supper and caught a few lightning bugs and then I came in the house and went upstairs to bed. I could hear Grandpa snoring the covers off so I knew that God wouldn't be around tonight. Then I saw some heat-lightning flash and then I thought that maybe he would do some more creating right in our yard. Grandma told me to go to sleep and if God started any creating outside my window she would come in and take care of it. That made me feel better and I guess I went to sleep.

The next day was the day that my father fell off the roof. The reason that he fell off the roof was because he was up there fixing the aerial for the radio which the lightning had knocked down last night only I didn't hear or see it. Grandma told me that she was sitting down-stairs in the parlor when the lightning struck and the flash came right down the chimney and the fireplace and hit Steamer the dog. She said it looked like his tail lit up and he yelped once and ran under the piano. And I don't blame him. But anyway my father fell off the roof and almost landed on Mr. Isaac Storm who was chopping down the old oak tree which got split by the lightning too. My father didn't fall very far because he landed on the back porch roof first. I thought that he looked funny sliding down on his behinder. He would put his hands down to stop himself and he would start getting slivers and then he would cuss and try to dig his feet into the shingles and that didn't stop him because he had on leather heels. He came down kind of slow-like and he couldn't do a thing about it but thump off on to the back porch roof and keep on sliding and then he came down the last part to the ground real fast just as Mr. Storm was going by with an armful of long branches that he had sawn off the oak tree. My father lit right in the middle of them and knocked him down too. Mr. Storm and my father both started cussing and Grandma came out on the back porch to see what was going on and she saw my father getting himself out of the branches, and he was all scratched up.

Was my father mad! He had one foot all tangled up in some aerial wire that came down with him and when he landed the wire got tight at the other end and pulled the pole down again so my father said, "To hell with it." Then he went out in back and started the car and drove away and didn't come back until supper time which was about the time that he usually came back from the store anyway, even when he didn't fall off the roof. When he came back he had a bandage on his wrist and he walked sort of stiff, which I guess he was. He said at supper that he would get Jerry Hall to come up and fix the damned aerial so that Grandma could hear Mr. Swindell play the organ on WOC Davenport. Finally he did come and we got to hear him play but there was a lot of static and it wasn't so good. My father also said that he knew why our Lord didn't remain a carpenter because he was too smart a man to climb roofs and fix poles.

Mr. Storm finished taking down the tree this week and he had Mr. Lincoln Cardwell to help him. Mr. Cardwell took down the wire that ran around the tree and had the other end fastened to the corner of the house near the bay window. Grandma put this heavy wire up to keep people, especially big boys, from cutting across her lawn. She would tie pieces of rag to it so that people could see the wire easier and maybe remember that it was there and not cut across her lawn. Last Hallowe'en she took the rags off when it got dark out and she and I sat in the bay window in the dark and waited for some boys to cut across her lawn, which they did. I saw Harry Harvey come across running fast and that wire hit him just above the knees and he made a circle in the air before coming down with a "whump." In a minute he got up and limped away. And I should think that he would. People didn't fool around with Grandma.

Only the police did once, and that was on the same Hallowe'en, only earlier in the evening, before the big boys were out doing tricks. It was when we smaller boys were out doing our tricks. We were down at Trowbridge's corner scaring some little girls who were carrying lighted pumpkins and wearing masks. Then a ghost in a white sheet came around the corner and ran at us and we were scared and started to run home. Just then the police wagon came along and saw the ghost and one of the policemen got out and grabbed the ghost and the sheet was ripped off and it was Grandma under it. Then we really were scared because we didn't know what Grandma would do to that policeman. And they both started laughing and she got in the police wagon and they gave her a ride home and she got there before I did, which was probably just as well anyway because my mother and my father would never have believed it if I had told them that the police had Grandma.

She invited the policeman in, and the driver too, and we all had coffee and cake and cider only I had cider and a doughnut besides, but no coffee. Then the policemen went out again to catch some more ghosts. Ha ha.

My mother said that she was terribly embarrassed and Grandpa wanted to know where Edna was and when would Jamie take him down to the City Hall. But it was real dark by this time, so Grandma and I sat in the bay window waiting for Harry Harvey. The policemen caught Grandma by mistake but Grandma caught Harry Harvey on purpose, which I suppose happens sometimes, even to policemen.

...CHOCOLATE CAKE CHURCH, CHERRY TREE LOVE, AND MC ARDLE'S OUTHOUSE...

THIS WAS THE SEPTEMBER THAT I STARTED DOING LOTS of things that I hadn't ever done before. I began school and I started Sunday school and I started going to church every Sunday too. My mother and my father both said it was a terrible thing to inflict church on a little boy and Grandma said, "Fiddlesticks." And that was the end of that.

I went to church with her. Anyway, my mother was the only alto in the choir and she could hold off six sopranos. My father said that when my mother died all the altos in the New Jerusalem would be out of a job and would have to take up harp playing. But my father was an usher so he stood in the back of the church and during the sermon he went out on the steps with George Hawley, the senior warden, and they smoked and talked while everybody else had to sit and listen to Mr. Garnett deliver his "tedious homily of love," as my father called it.

But I was in church and I didn't have to listen. When it came time for the sermon hymn, which was usually "Fling Out the Banner High and Wide," only sometimes it was "Holy Offerings Rich and Rare," unless the choir decided to do that one during the collection. When the sermon hymn started, Grandma would motion me to sit down on the kneeling bench and face the empty pew. Then she would hand me a piece of chocolate cake and the funny papers. All the time that the old people had to listen to Mr. Garnett's sermons I was looking at Old Doc Yak and Bobby Make–Believe and I didn't have to listen so it wasn't so bad for me or my father or Mr. Hawley. Just Grandma.

But I am ahead of my story which had to do with starting Sunday school, which was a very confusing affair. I started Sunday school for the first time last January on my birthday. I didn't like it very much and every time that I went I got sick and so I didn't have to go until I was bigger which was now when I started school and church officially.

I remember that first time because Mrs. Kent said that everybody who had a birthday had to come up to the table and put a penny in the glass bank with the slot on top for every birthday he ever had. I went up front and dropped in my five pennies one at a time and everybody counted out loud and then they sang, "Happy birthday to Jamie," and I had a penny left over because my father gave me six pennies.

But the next thing Mrs. Kent did was to go out in the kitchen and bring back a big turkey platter with a picture of Independence Hall painted on it in blue. Miss Cooper started playing "Praise God from Whom All Blessings Flow." We marched around the table and made our offering and Mrs. Kent led the singing and watched the pennies, and I gave my last penny and there wasn't any money to buy candy or gum for any of us because

Mrs. Kent and the Sunday school got all our money. That's the way it always was for me at church. I didn't like that idea very much. Then we sang another hymn to a pretty song. I thought it was called "Conrad's Sister's Shoulders" but Grandma told me later that it was "Onward, Christian Soldiers," and it did make more sense. I always did have trouble understanding Mrs. Kent, especially when she sang the "Marshall Aze," which she sang the Sunday after Bastille Day every year. I had a hard time understanding what "Bastille" was because we had bastille soap at home and I didn't think that it was anything to make a song about in church because that kind of soap hurt my eyes when it got in them. It was sort of dumb. My father said that the bastille was the city jail and I asked him why Mrs. Kent didn't go there and sing it because anyway she lived right across the street from the jail. My father laughed and said, "Forget it, son." But I didn't.

Virginia sits right behind me in school, which I started to go to last week. She is very pretty, which makes it hard for me to swallow sometimes. I think she looks like Grandma used to look when she was a little girl, but not like now because Grandma is wrinkled and has white hair and bunions. Virginia's hair is gold color. I saw a picture of Grandma when she was a little girl and she looked a lot different then from the way she looks now. Virginia smiles at me sometimes. My chest gets tight and, as I said, I can't swallow, and I can't think of anything to say. But she makes me feel good down inside.

She has a blue dress that whistles when she walks. I told Grandma about the whistling dress and she said that it was made of taffety. I asked her how a dress could be made of taffety, especially a blue one, because I didn't think Virginia's dress would taste like candy. Grandma explained to me that it was a different kind of taffety, and that when she was a little girl she had a blue taffety dress too, only it was longer than Virginia's and came down to her ankles, but it was for Sunday church only, and sometimes Christmas and Easter and Thanksgiving. No wonder Virginia is like Grandma was in olden times when darkness covered the earth and there wasn't as much firmament as there is now.

We went out to the playground at recess time. I gave her a piece of candy. It was a horehound drop with sugar on, only most of the sugar wore off in my pocket. There was a piece of white thread stuck to the horehound drop too. It looked like coconut but it wasn't. Just thread. I took the thread off and gave the candy to Virginia and she put it in her mouth and told me that I mustn't tell her mother because her mother wouldn't like it. Her mother told her that she must not take candy from men or people that loitered around playgrounds. But she did and she smiled at me and I got that funny feeling in my chest. Then the bell rang and we went back in the school room and she sat down behind me.

Virginia's house was near mine, so I walked home with her and Paul, only Paul's house was closer to the school, so we went by his house first and Virginia and I went on to her house and each of us had a cookie and then we went out in the backyard and climbed in the cherry tree. When I climbed up higher than Virginia I could see my house across the vacant lot beyond Mc-Ardle's house which was next door. The cherry tree didn't grow high enough for me to see over the top of

McArdle's house but just over the lilac bush which was in the way and which I had to walk around in order to take the shortcut home when I was ready to go, only I wasn't ready to go yet.

When I was way up high I looked down at Virginia and she looked up at me and smiled and said that she thought I was brave to be up so high. I thought so too, then my foot slipped and I fell a long way. My foot got caught in the crotch of the cherry tree and swung me around and left me hanging upside down and I couldn't get up or down and I was in a mess. Virginia could do something, and she did. She climbed down past me and got to the ground without falling and ran in the house to get her mother but she had gone to the neighbor's house and there wasn't anyone to help. So Virginia came back and told me. My face was near her face only mine was upside down. She said that she would run over to McArdle's house and get somebody to help get me out of the tree and for me to stay right there and not be afraid because she would come right back. Then she kissed me on the cheek and my face burned even more than for just being upside down, and she ran to McArdle's house. I felt better, even being upside down, except that my ankle hurt and was getting swollen. So I tried to get down out of the tree again but that made it hurt more, so I hung upside down and watched the clouds on the blue ground and sometimes looked at the green sky.

She came back right away and Mrs. McArdle trotting along behind her. Mrs. McArdle was hanging out the wash which she did for neighbors because the McArdles were poor, and Mr. McArdle couldn't work all the time because sometimes he was drunk, which was often.

Grandma told me and that is so. Well, when Virginia told Mrs. McArdle about me being upside down in the cherry tree she came running and laughing, but it wasn't funny. Mr. McArdle heard all the laughing and commotion and he staggered out on their back porch and hung on to the railing, trying to figure out what was going on and watching Mrs. McArdle untangle me from the cherry tree. Then Mr. McArdle decided to come over and help but he missed the top step and fell all the way to the bottom and landed in a basket of clean clothes and tipped it over and all the chickens squawked and ran into the bushes. Mrs. McArdle stood me right-side-up on the ground and ran back into her yard and was yelling at Dan (that's Mr. McArdle), and he was trying to get up but couldn't do it very good. She picked up a clothespole and beat him over the head with it and it broke. He tried to get up again and get away from the beating which she was doing better now because the pole was shorter and she could swing it faster. Every time he would get up she would slug him with the short pole and down he'd go.

Mrs. McArdle called for her brother, Paddy, and he came out of the house and the two of them took Mr. McArdle and dragged him over to the outhouse and shoved him inside and slammed the door and locked it from the outside so he couldn't get out and muss up any more washing. Mr. McArdle started banging on the inside door of the outhouse and he was cussing Paddy and called him the seventh son of an Irish hoar, whatever that was. I asked Grandma about that when I got home and she said that it was something that Irishmen thought other Irishmen were sometimes, especially when they got mad.

Well, Paddy picked up a brick which was used to prop up the clothespole and he threw it against the outhouse and Dan stopped yelling and Paddy went back in the house and Mrs. McArdle went back to hanging the wash.

All the time of this excitement I sat on the ground and watched everything. Virginia kneeled down beside me and rubbed my ankle. Pretty soon it felt better and I got up and we went into her house and she gave me a cookie and took one herself. We laughed about Mr. McArdle falling in that wash basket, but getting hit on the head with the clothespole so hard that it broke wasn't funny. I wouldn't want to get hit like that or especially get locked in an outhouse either.

I heard Grandma calling for me so I told Virginia that I thought that I ought to go home now, but I didn't really want to, but I had to go to the bathroom. As I started across the McArdles' backyard to get to my backyard I walked past the outhouse where Mr. McArdle was locked up. It was quiet now. Paddy had gone back in the house and gone to sleep and Mrs. McArdle could be heard washing clothes in the cellar and I could hear Mr. McArdle sort of moaning and crying like. So I went up to the outhouse door and I asked Mr. McArdle if there was anything the matter.

In a quiet, low voice Mr. McArdle said, "Thank you, son. Now if you will unlatch that door I believe that I will come out and lie down in the shade of that apple tree. And it's a fine lad you are, helping an old man who isn't feelin' well." So I reached up and unhooked the hook and Mr. McArdle came out and stumbled over to the apple tree and lay down. But first he put the hook back on the outhouse door and then he went over and lay down and I went home and Mr. McArdle went to sleep and everything was quiet again.

I like Virginia a lot, and we have good times together, except after I get up in a tree and get that funny feeling when she smiles at me and that makes me slip and fall. Virginia is good to me, and I think she likes me too. I even think I like Mr. McArdle, but he smells funny most of the time. Mrs. McArdle sure whacked him with that clothespole. I bet she is tired and has to go and lie down for awhile before finishing the wash.

...YELLOW HAIR, BLACK HAIR, GOLDEN HAIR, BUMBLEBEES, CATFISH, AND ANTS...

The man who bosses the teachers and runs the school and rings the bell for recess with a button that he pushes alongside his desk came into our room today. He took Virginia and Evelyn and me with him to his office, which is how I found out about where the playground bell rang from and who did it. It was Mr. Potter all the time except when he was down in the furnace room arguing with the janitor, Mr. Corbin, who had a cot down there alongside the boiler because he wasn't feeling very good much of the time and had to lie down often because he was also very old and bent over. Grandma said that's what happened if you pushed a broom too long and the devil didn't empty your hands of work, ever, but that's what one could expect in this Land of Whoa where trouble is sent to try us.

Well, anyway, on the way to Mr. Potter's office I tried to remember what I had done that was bad and I couldn't think of anything special that he would know about even if he is a smart man, because I always went straight home from school except that I stopped off at Virginia's house, unless she was going to her piano lesson, in which case I played with Freddie and Todd in the empty lot next door.

When we got to his office he sat down in a big chair that was on the end of a long screw. The chair could swing around and I watched the screw go up in the chair and I wondered if it went into Mr. Potter, but when he stood up I could see that it hadn't gone through the seat yet. I wondered about that. Mr. Potter lined the three of us up in front of him and Evelyn began to cry and he said there was nothing to cry about because we had been good students. He leaned forward and Evelyn stopped crying and Mr. Potter folded his hands together across his stomach and told us that we were too smart for the first grade with all those Irish kids in there throwing things and the boys pulling the girls' braids, so he was going to put us in another room with a new teacher. We went back out of the office, and that was when I noticed that the screw didn't come through the chair into Mr. Potter's big behinder. We marched past the big clock and the firegong which Mr. Corbin pulled the rope of when there was fire drill and on past the water fountain where Charley McGonigle threw up once when he came back from recess. We went right into Miss Vinnegard's room and Mr. Potter explained everything to her and all the kids looked at us and Katie Muldoon stuck out her tongue at Virginia and called her a dirty Protestant and Miss Vinnegard said, "That will do, Kathleen," and she stopped but kept sticking her tongue out when the teacher wasn't looking. This room had as many Irish kids as the first grade only they were the bigger brothers and sisters. I knew some of them, but I didn't play with them because they were too big and too tough for me, except Danny McArdle who was my size but a year older, and who was in this room and he waved at me and smacked Katie

Muldoon alongside the head and pulled her braid.

Miss Vinnegard had bright yellow hair that looked like it came out of a packing box. It was cut in a Buster Brown bob, just like mine only my hair is black. She smiled all the time and nodded her head and she was kind of heavy. She had two round spots on her cheeks that were bright red, and her eyes were bright blue. She wore a middy blouse, like my mother did sometimes. And she had a blue skirt and big tan shoes with square toes, and she kept nodding her head up and down and smiling all the time that Mr. Potter was in the room and was talking. Miss Vinnegard looked like that great big rag doll which was in the store window of the Bee Hive Department Store at Christmas.

Mr. Potter finished talking to Miss Vinnegard and she stopped nodding and smiling and Mr. Potter said goodby and he went back to the office to get ready to ring the bell for recess when it was time. Miss Vinnegard showed Virginia and Evelyn and me where to sit, and we sat. Virginia had a seat over by the window, and she made Evelyn sit in front of me, and I was right behind her, and all the kids looked at us and that made me feel sort of full and like they didn't want me there, except Danny McArdle and Franklin Finnegan who were hitting each other when Miss Vinnegard was looking the other way and smiling at somebody else.

But I didn't care because Virginia was there and she would look over at me and smile sometimes. When she would look up suddenly from her work she would catch me looking at her and then I would look at the ceiling and try to swallow and pretend that I was interested in what that fly was doing and how he could turn over in the air and land upside down on the ceiling and not get dizzy or fall off.

I could play with Virginia at recess too, which I did after Mr. Potter rang the bell. Then when he rang the bell again we went back into the building. I got there first so I could watch Virginia walk by my desk and hear the taffety dress whistle when she wore it which was nearly every day except sometimes a pink dress which didn't whistle but wrinkled instead. Virginia would smile at me again and I would get that funny feeling in my chest and I felt good all over until Katie Muldoon called Virginia a dirty Protestant and I wanted to hit her one on the head but she was two rows over and one back and I couldn't reach her.

Evelyn's black braids were almost always on my desk. I used to watch them and admire them and sometimes touch them. Then I would forget about school. Miss Vinnegard would watch me and forget what she was talking about and then she would catch me touching Evelyn's hair and she would call me up to her desk and scold me quietly so nobody could hear. She would tell me to leave Evelyn's hair alone, but that was a very hard thing to do because it was so shiny and it had a red color in it when I turned the braid in the sunlight. Besides, I like to touch it and I didn't intend not to touch it any more. Evelyn didn't have any feeling in her hair so I didn't think it would matter. All the feeling was in the ends of my fingers and through my eyeballs, so I didn't tell Miss Vinnegard what I was thinking about the whole thing, but made a false promise not to, which was like the time that I told my mother that I was sorry when I really wasn't and I got to have Christmas.

Once I was holding the braid after Miss Vinnegard told me not to, but she was looking the other way telling Katie Muldoon that "That will do, Kathleen." Evelyn turned quickly, not knowing that I had hold of her braid, and it jerked her head back and then she knew I held her hair. She was mad at me. All I was doing was holding her hair and turning it in the light to see it change color. It was very beautiful and looked alive sometimes. But Miss Vinnegard and Evelyn didn't think so.

Right there in front of everybody Evelyn yelled at me and said that she hated boys, especially me, because her mother told her never to let a boy touch her because something terrible might happen, and it did, and that boys wet the bed and picked their noses and they were dirty, and now look what I had done and now she would have to wash her hair. Franklin Finnegan said, "Shut up, ya dirty Protestant. Jamie ain't hurtin' ya any." Then he hit her with a wet paper wad that he shot out of a rubber band on his thumb and everybody laughed but Miss Vinnegard, who said, "That will do, Franklin. That will do, Evelyn. That will do, James."

After that she kept her hair off my desk and I learned to read better. But that wasn't until Miss Vinnegard moved me to the front desk where I had Rose O'Leary behind me. If she had to sit anywhere I guess behind me was the best because she wasn't pretty and had orange hair and her round, fat face was almost one solid freckle.

Evelyn wasn't very pretty either, and besides she was too bossy and she let her tongue get away from her and it was wagging her into hell. That's the way Grandma put it when I told her. Evelyn's lips were tight and skinny and there wasn't any blood in them, I could tell. She didn't have a pretty mouth like Virginia. Her face was sort of pinched up as if her seat itched all the time, which I don't suppose it did really, but looked like it should. When she smiled her face had a crooked crack in it like that lady in the stained-glass window that cracked when I was a little boy. She was skinny too, and that didn't help matters. I didn't like Evelyn except for her hair that changed color in the sunlight, and that was beautiful, even if it was black Protestant hair, like Katie Muldoon said. Katie should talk.

I wished sometimes Virginia had Evelyn's hair, but then she would be so pretty that I couldn't stand it. Her hair was gold and it was pretty too, but it didn't change color, but Virginia couldn't help that. That was all right, because Virginia had a beautiful mouth especially when she smiled at me and even the Irish kids liked her sparkling blue eyes and the dress that whistled when she walked. But I was the only one that she had kissed and I was upside down in the cherry tree at the time. I liked Virginia. She always made me feel good, and her mother always had cookies for me too.

Paul and Virginia and Freddie and I started walking home after school one day and Franklin Finnegan caught up with us and he had his pet bumblebee with him that he kept in a cleaned-out peanut butter jar with holes punched in the top so that the bee could breathe and we could hear him buzz. Mr. Finnegan, Franklin's father, had taken some thread and tied it around the bumblebee's hind leg. Then Franklin could let the bee out of the jar on a long line of thread and he could get his exercise. We all liked to watch the bumblebee fly with that thread on his leg and then listen to him buzz when he got angry when Franklin would reel him back in. Virginia wasn't too keen about the bumblebee, but she was brave about it and pretty soon Franklin went in his house which was only a block away from school on our way home.

Freddie told us that his Uncle Bud had caught a great big catfish and put it in the bathtub until his mother found out about it on Saturday and made him take it out. So Uncle Bud had to give the catfish to Mr. Lincoln Cardwell, the colored man, who lives back of the water tank with Mrs. Cardwell, who mops the floor at the bank and has hollyhocks and watermelons and pumpkins in her corn patch. So we didn't get to see the big catfish. I have seen them before, but never in a bathtub, which I think is most unusual, especially for a catfish who belongs in a muddy river or in a frying pan and not a bathtub.

Mr. Cardwell was the man who got all the wood from the oak tree that Mr. Storm sawed down the day that my father fell off the roof. The two of them got a pail full of ants, too, out of the old tree. Mr. Cardwell put some sawdust in the pail and put some kerosene on it and set fire to it and burned all the ants. The ants that were left over, and the ones that got out of the pail, were all upset, losing their home and their friends and all. I felt sorry for them.

...UNCLE CHARLIE, MY FATHER, AND THE JUDGE...

IT WAS SATURDAY SO THERE WASN'T ANY SCHOOL. BUT IT was raining and I couldn't go outdoors to play. Besides, all the Irish kids were up at Father Foley's church having the catechism pounded into their heads and there wasn't anybody to play with anyway except Freddie and Paul. Freddie was out on Grandpa Schirmer's ranch and Paul was down at his grandpa's feed barn brushing the funeral horses because he told me that they were going to hitch them all up to the hacks and drive people to the cemetery to see Mrs. Hander get buried. I would like to see that myself because Mrs. Hander was a fat woman and my father said that her name should have been Mrs. Hinder, and I laughed, and Grandma said that the Lord made all kinds of people and we should thank him that he didn't make us any different than he did because it could have been worse, like having buck teeth as big as Fay Ortgeiser's who lived down by Mr. Storm's cottage by the ravine where the goldenrod was that made people sneeze in summer. When Miss Ortgeiser got ready to sneeze she reared back her head and curled her lip like one of Ben Baus's horses when he didn't want to pull the funeral carriage. My father said that Fay was sure set up to be the world's champion corn-on-the-cob eater.

Well, anyway, Grandma was sitting in the bay window darning socks where she could look out and I stood there in the window and looked out too. Who should come stumbling down the street but Judge Clabhorn. The judge was an old man with a full white beard and a tall hat and Grandma called him disgusting. He lived a block beyond our house, next to Deckers and across from the cemetery and sometimes the judge would get drunk, but not the same way as Mr. McArdle. The judge was always very dignified, and walked slowly as he weaved back and forth across the sidewalk on his way down to the Courthouse which was three blocks down the hill toward town and across from the Presbyterian church and Mr. Staples' funeral home.

Today was one of his days. At least that is what Grandma said. It was even more than that, I thought, because the judge didn't have any trousers on. As I said, he had on his high hat and his swallowtail coat and a shirt and a tie and a wing collar and shoes. Under all that he had on his long underwear and his garters, and he didn't seem to miss his trousers. He also carried a cane and kept his left hand up under his whiskers with the back-side-up and walked along back and forth across the sidewalk and tried to keep his balance. He always held his head high and looked very sedate and gentlemanly.

There was a hitching post at our curb and it was a big one with two rings in it which were held by a horse's head on the end of the post. Well, Judge Clabhorn came lurching along and he saw that hitching post and I guess he thought that it was somebody that he knew because he took his hand out from under his whiskers and started over to the hitching post, and he couldn't stop and he bumped right into it. Then he backed away and bowed deeply and tipped his hat to it and went on down the street.

And Mother came and watched and she said, "Well! Did you ever?" and Grandma said, "I never did." And they both clucked and then Grandma said, "Jamie, I think that we had better pray for Judge Clabhorn today. And all the people who will be in Court."

My father, who had watched the whole scene from the upstairs bedroom window and now came down the stairs laughing, said that today is Saturday and that there isn't any court today and that the judge is going down to the Ideal Cafe for his morning coffee and then probably go over to Kelly's saloon and hold court there without his pants. My father said, "No breakfast for me. I'm going downtown about a block behind the judge and watch the fun when he goes by the Methodist parsonage and when his friends see him at the Ideal Cafe without his pants." My father went out the door still laughing.

Grandma put the darning in her lap and bowed her head and my mother went back out to the kitchen without saying anything and I stayed there and bowed my head with Grandma, and she prayed silently for a long time. Then she got a little louder and I could hear the end of the prayer which went, ". . . and so, O Lord, save this man from the evils of his drunken days that he may mete out justice and know what he is doing. Have mercy on the judge, Lord, as he would do if he were you and you were him, and he was sober, and then he wouldn't be disgusting but a fine and upright citizen and minister of the law tempered with mercy, as thou art. Amen."

I thought that Grandma's prayer would certainly be thought over by the Lord, if he was anywhere around here on a rainy Saturday, and maybe he would do something about it by Monday morning, Sunday being the Lord's Day to rest from his labors no matter what might come up. Monday he'd fix everything he had a mind to. Grandma said so.

My grandma told me the following Friday that Uncle Charlie was going to visit us for the weekend and that he was coming on the Corn King Limited on the Northwestern Railroad which arrived at 8:40 P.M. every night, and that we would all go up to meet the train. My father said that if I was a good boy the rest of the day and all the next day then we would drive up to the station in time to see the 8:07 train, which was a local. My father said that "local" meant that it stopped at every high fence where there was an outhouse, but I bet he was fooling me, because if the train did that between here and Chicago there would be eleven stops between here and Franklin Grove, including Nachusa Station, and it would never get to Chicago.

Every time that Uncle Charlie came out for a visit he always brought along some furniture in the baggage car. His wife, who was my grandma's sister, had died in her sleep of too much morphine and how she got it while she was sleeping I don't know. My father, being a druggist, said that she was in a dream world most of the time anyway and that she found it a pretty good place. Then he said out loud to himself that these days he can't afford to have his own garden of dreams any more but sells them to other people, and he doesn't take trips except to Chicago once in a while and the rest of the time he works around the store and lets his mind wander. Grandma said that he ought to be ashamed of himself for talking like that.

For a moment she got angry with him for talking about her sister who had gone to her reward in heaven and couldn't defend herself. Grandma called my father a Pharisee and he said that his best customers were Pharisees, and besides that, Grandpa was treasurer of the parish and that made him a money-changer in the temple. And Grandma turned away and said to my mother, "That man!"

And Mother said, "Did you ever?" And Grandma said that she never did. Then they carried the supper dishes out to the kitchen and my father went to the hall and put on his straw hat with the red band and he slammed the screen door quietly and started down the street to go back to the store because there might be somebody down there who might want to buy a stamp or use the telephone and call Hong Kong. Anyway, that's what he told me.

Grandma got over her mad by the time that the dishes were done and she thought that she would play a joke on my father, so she called him on the phone. She held the receiver away from her ear so that my mother and I could hear.

The phone rang three times, then my father answered, "Passmore Pharmacy. May I help you, please?" He sounded most pleasant, but of course he didn't know that Grandma was on the other end and maybe he was still mad.

Grandma tried to change her voice by putting a spoon in her mouth and then talking real deep. She said, "Can you tell me if the street car has gone around the corner yet?"

My father said that he would take a look, which I suppose he did because he was gone for awhile. Then he came back and said, "It's coming down the track now."

Grandma said, "Which way is it going?"

Then my father caught on that he was being fooled but he didn't know who was doing the fooling yet. He answered and said, "Straight ahead to the cemetery and it's too bad you missed it. There will be another one along in twenty minutes going the other way to the casket factory. Maybe you can get that one." And he hung up.

And Grandma and I laughed and laughed. And my mother said, "Did you ever?" And Grandma said that she never did. And then she called my father back and told him that she was the one that had made the call and they both laughed and nobody was mad at anybody any more and everybody was ready to be pleasant all weekend when Uncle Charlie was there.

Uncle Charlie was an old man with a big bay window which shook when he laughed, only Uncle Charlie didn't laugh very often. He had a big red nose that looked like a Christmas tree bulb and his eyes were weepy and he was always wiping them and then touching the ends of his curved mustache with the handkerchief before putting it back in his pocket. My father said that Uncle Charlie looked like a bloodhound that has lost his scent. But he didn't say that in front of Grandma you bet, because she thought that Uncle Charlie was a fine fellow. And so did I. But he was forgetful sometimes, like on the Fourth of July when he visited us. He threw away the match and held on to the firecracker and it nearly blew his thumb off. Grandma rushed him into the house and put a bandage on it and then Uncle Charlie went to his room for a long time and when he came out he turned the wrong way in the upstairs hall and couldn't find the stairs. He stumbled into Grandpa's room and Grandpa asked him where Edna was, and Uncle Charlie acted a little bit like Judge Clabhorn the day that he apologized to the hitching post. And then we had supper and skyrockets but Uncle Charlie sat in the porch swing with Mrs. Dement and didn't say much, but he didn't have a chance anyway.

This weekend was his first visit since the Fourth of July and we all went up to meet him when he came in and I got to see the 8:07 first, and then that went down the track with a big noise and sparks coming out of the smokestack and we waited around for the Corn King Limited and my father took me down to the spur track where the switch engine slept all night and sure enough there it was, only Cassius McClanahan was home with his family I guess. And so was the fireman, Lumpy Lambert, and nobody was around. So my father lifted me up into the cab and I sat where Cassius McClanahan sat when he ran the locomotive and I put my elbow on the arm rest like he did and I pretended that I was on my way to the cement plant for some chopped rock, only I really wasn't, but I thought so at the time. Then I heard the long whistle of the Corn King Limited as it came under the Peoria Avenue Bridge so that everybody would know that it was on time, which it was.

And there was Uncle Charlie and everybody was glad to see him, and my father said, "Hello, Howard," to the conductor and they shook hands. While Grandma and my mother were greeting Uncle Charlie my father said

71

that he would check out the baggage up ahead, so he and I went up. And I got to go in the big locomotive where Chet Ramsey was the engineer. It was a big live locomotive. It was noisy and hot and puffing, and the fireman opened the fire door and threw in some coal and I watched him. Then we got down and went to the baggage car and there was some more of Uncle Charlie's furniture, including a dresser that had eight drawers and was almost as high as the bank building downtown only it didn't have windows or an elevator. My father said Bill Dauntler would be up in the morning with his dray team and haul the furniture up to our house after the horses had a good night's sleep and were full of morning oats. I get oats in the morning, too, but not in a feed bag, and besides mine are cooked and have cream and sugar on them and strawberries sometimes in June. But I guess that it doesn't make that much difference to the horses. They didn't know what they were missing anyway, so I guess it was O.K. But I'd rather have oatmeal and strawberries.

The next day when Mr. Dauntler drove the team and the wagon to our house I remembered that song that Grandma sings about the Land of Whoa and I wondered what a horse thought about it. Horses think. The team was looking at me when Mr. Dauntler was unloading the furniture, and I looked at the team and one of them turned to the other and whinnied and I wondered what he said, so I tried to be friendly with both horses but neither of them said anything more but just stood there and waited and kept moving the flies around their hams by swinging their tails back and forth, which I should think would make a nervous wreck out of a fly.

Then Uncle Charlie and I walked downtown and everybody that we would meet would say hello to Uncle Charlie and he would try to remember their names so that he could call them by their right name. When he would see somebody coming he would quick ask me who they were and I would tell him because I knew everybody. We had gotten down to the corner of Main Street and Galena Avenue and along came Mr. Staples, the undertaker, who looked at Uncle Charlie like he knew him and that maybe he was expecting him. And Uncle Charlie asked me who the man was and I told him that it was Mr. Staples.

So Uncle Charlie went up to Mr. Staples just as though he had known him all his life, which he hadn't. Uncle Charlie said, "Well, well, if it isn't Joe Staples. And how is business, Joe?" I hadn't told Uncle Charlie that Mr. Staples was an undertaker and worked with God when he called people home. And Mr. Staples coughed and said that business was just fine, and we went one way and Mr. Staples went off in another, probably on his way to another body that needed shipment to the New Jerusalem, as my father always said.

When we got home that afternoon Uncle Charlie went to his room for a long time but came down in time for supper, but he got lost on the second floor again and was having a visit with Grandpa who thought he was in Peoria. Uncle Charlie was very talkative all through supper as he was telling us about Big Bill Thompson, the mayor of Chicago, who was helping Uncle Charlie stay sober and maybe one day he would be mayor. My father got to laughing and turned it very quickly into a coughing spell because my mother and Grandma glared at him as

Uncle Charlie kept on talking about what a fine fellow Big Bill was, and J. Hamilton Lewis, too, who was a senator down in Washington and had red whiskers and was a Democrat and everybody around our house was a Republican, including Uncle Charlie. Except Grandma wasn't because she said that she voted for that man Wilson. My father just sat there and drank his coffee black, which was unusual because he always put cream in it when he wasn't upset.

After dinner we all went into the parlor and Uncle Charlie reached in his pocket and pulled out a paper roll of fifty pennies and he took the paper off and he threw the pennies in the air and I scrambled to get as many as I could. I forgot to say that Freddie and Franklin Finnegan were there too. They were waiting for me to finish supper so that we could go out and play. It was funny how they always came to see me when Uncle Charlie was visiting our house. I got twenty-three pennies and Freddie got seventeen and Franklin got ten and a dime that got in the penny shower by mistake. So we went down to Finalli's Ice Cream Parlor and got a treat. It always happened when Uncle Charlie visited our house.

...PAGEANTS, BUNNY HATS, AND ESSAYS... RECEETS TOO...

Miss Cooper told our Sunday school class today that each one of us would be in the Christmas pageant. She said that she had gone downtown to see Mr. Mathias at the Golden Rule grocery store and he gave her six burlap bags that potatoes came in and that she took them home and washed the potato dust out of them and would give them to our mothers to make shepherd suits out of.

Last Christmas I was a member of the heavenly host and wore an angel suit that my mother made me. It was all white and had tinsel sewed around the ends of the sleeves and around the collar. Miss Scanlon made ten pair of wings. She made them with paper pie plates and stuck them together so they look more like fish scales to me, and my father laughed and said I looked like a landed fish. Being a member of the heavenly host meant that I walked down the aisle with the other angels carrying a lighted candle. The lighted candle was pushed through the bottom of a paper cup which acted as a tallow catcher so that the stuff wouldn't fall on the carpet. But Dickie Drummond bumped me twice and I got hot tallow on the back of my hand and that made me jump and I spilled tallow on the carpet. The next day after

Christmas Dickie's mother and my mother went down to the church to take the tallow off the carpet. There were a lot more tallow spots than I made, but our mothers had to take them all off the carpet. It was interesting to watch them do it. They brought along some ink blotters and two irons. They heated the irons on the stove in the kitchen in the basement and ran upstairs with them while they were still hot and they put a blotter down on top of a spot of tallow and put the iron on the blotter and held it there a minute and when they took it up the tallow had melted into the blotter and left the carpet clean. I thought that was a good way to do it. I would never have thought of it. I don't think that Dickie's mother or my mother thought of it by themselves either. I bet they asked Grandma and she knew and she told them because she had it written down somewhere, like her receet for washing clothes which she told me that she got from her mother, which was my great-grandmother that fell down the back stairs when she was an old lady and the Lord and Mr. Staples called her home.

Grandma said that she knew the receet by heart and that she would give it to me to keep in a box so that when I grew up I would know how things were done in the old days, which she did, and which I did, and here it is.

1. Build fire in backyard to heat kettle of rainwater.
2. Set tubs so smoke won't blow in eyes if wind perks.
3. Shave one cake lye soap in boiling water.
4. Sort things. Make three piles. One white. One colored. One work britches and rags.

5. Stir flour in cold water til smooth then thin
   down with boiling water.
6. Rub dirty spots on board. Scrub hard then
   boil.
7. Rub colored but don't boil. Rench and
   sturch.
8. Take white things out of kettle with broom-
   stick handle. Rench blue and sturch.
9. Spread dish towels on grass. Hang old
   rags on fence.
10. Pore rench water on flower bed.
11. Scrub porch with hot sopy water.
12. Turn tubs upside down.
13. Go put on clean dress. Smooth hair. Make
    cup of tea.
14. Set and rest and rock awhile. Hum hymns.
    Count blessings.

Grandma couldn't spell very well and sometimes she'd read to me out of a book, which she did when I was real little, only most of the time she just told me stories which were pretty good. Grandma only went through fourth grade and learned how to read the Bible and the *Book of Common Prayer* and the *Methodist Almanac* which explained how to do things that her mother forgot to tell her when she was little. Grandma said that all anybody needed to know was in those three books and that anything else one read was the same stuff done over again and not written as plain as the Bible, the *Book of Common Prayer*, and the *Methodist Almanac*. I asked her about the hymn book, and she said all the ideas in the hymn book came out of the Bible in the first place and were set to music so that was different.

Sometimes I forget where I am when I am writing these things down because I get to thinking about something Grandma said instead of what Miss Cooper tells us in Sunday school. Well, when all the gunny sacks had been passed out I didn't get one. I felt pretty bad about it until Miss Cooper said that I was going to be a wise man and I wouldn't wear a burlap bag made over into a shepherd suit but that I could wear my new bathrobe and instead of the belt on the bathrobe they would wrap a strip of tinsel around my middle and make me a paper crown covered with silver paper. Miss Scanlon said that she had a Buddha incense burner that I could carry which I would leave at the crib as a Christmas present to the Christ child.

When I told Grandma that I was going to carry the smoke on Christmas Eve she didn't like the idea very much. I told her that I wouldn't spill any smoke on the carpet like I did the tallow last year and besides I was bigger now. She said that wasn't what bothered her, but what did was having incense in church. She said that although she liked the smell of incense it wasn't the sort of thing that one ought to be smelling in church, and that you shouldn't do it on the Lord's Day especially.

I wondered about that because sometimes on Sunday morning Mr. Garnett starts off the service by saying "Let my prayer be set forth in thy sight as the incense, and let the lifting up of my hands be an evening sacrifice." Grandma said, "Mr. Garnett said no such thing at Morning Prayer."

Then I said, "Well, I bet he said it at Evening Prayer, then," and Grandma looked it up in the *Book of Common Prayer*, and there it was.

Grandma said, "You are getting too big for your britches, catching your old grandma like that." And I felt pretty big.

While we were on the subject I thought that it would be a good time to ask her about Mrs. Cheadle and the psalm about the pelican. So I did.

"Grandma," I said, "what does that psalm mean which Mrs. Cheadle says so loud right behind us in church? You know. 'I am like a pelican in my wickedness.' How can a pelican be wicked?"

She laughed and told me that Mrs. Cheadle needed her glasses changed and besides she read so slowly that she read the psalm when everybody else was through, and what the psalm really said was, "I am like the pelican in the wilderness."

That explanation was a little better but still confusing, so I asked her what *that* meant, and she told me.

"Over in the Holy Land the pelicans lived along the shore of the Mediterranean Sea so that they could catch fish to eat. Sometimes a bad thunderstorm would come up and the wind would blow, and if a pelican was flying at the time then the wind would catch him and blow him away from the sea and he would land on the desert of Moab, beyond the Dead Sea, which was the wilderness. And there were no fish there, so he didn't have anything to eat, and he was all alone and didn't have any of his friends, and it was like a foreign country." Grandma explained that sometimes people are like that pelican. They get blown off course and they don't know how to get back to their friends and where they would rather live and they get as lonely as a pelican in their own wilderness. And all that finally made sense. I wish that it would to Mrs. Cheadle, but maybe she did feel like a pelican in her wickedness. I don't really know. Grandma said she would ask Mrs. Cheadle.

I thought that the Christmas pageant came off all right, but Grandma didn't like the incense. She said it came from the heathen Chinee, whoever they are. Besides she said that the confusion up around the altar with the whole Sunday school up there setting each other on fire was dreadful. She said that Christmas Eve at our church was as confusing as Pentecost, and I asked her what that was, and she said that was the birthday of the church.

"Were there any candles?" I asked.

"I don't think so," said Grandma, "but people were running around in the streets and talking different languages just like the holy rollers and everything was in chaos. It was the most disordered day in the history of the church, and I am pleased to note that St. Paul got them all calmed down when he came along." After that we changed the subject. I thought of asking her why St. Paul wrote so many letters that nobody could understand and then I thought maybe I wouldn't ask. So I didn't.

When I was a little boy I remember that for a long time I thought that God had five sons. They were Abraham and Moses and Noah and David and Only-Forgotten, the one we believed in. But Grandma straightened me out on that when she got through laughing about it. And it did sound kind of funny, now that I remember it.

Something else that used to bother me was the size of Abraham's bosom. Lazarus and sometimes other people were either falling on or being enfolded by it. It must have been something, even bigger than the pillow lady at the hospital, or Mrs. Dement. My father said that Mrs. Dement reminded him of a pouter pigeon. And she did me too. Sort of. But I didn't know for sure about Abraham, and I didn't for a long time. Except pouter pigeons don't talk as loud or as often as Mrs. Dement, and that is a good thing.

As long as we are on the subject, there are a couple of other things which bothered me because it was a long time before I understood. There used to be a soprano in the choir and her name was "Rosanna." On the first Sunday of the month, when we had Holy Communion, the choir would sing, "Holy, holy, holy, Lord God of hosts," and they would end with "Rosanna on the highest." I used to wonder about that because Rosanna *was* always on the highest note. One day I was singing that song around the house and Grandma corrected me and said that it was, "*Ho*sanna *in* the highest." When I asked her who "Hosanna" was, she said that it wasn't anybody in particular, but that it meant, "Hurray for the Lord." And that made a lot more sense.

As long as we were talking about things that had me mixed up, I asked her why the children in the Sunday school wore skull caps with rabbit ears on them on Easter Day. Grandma thought awhile, and she said, "You mean those Easter bunny hats."

I said, "Yes."

She answered, "They are the most stupid and preposterous hats I ever saw, and outrageous, too. Rabbits indeed! And on Easter! Nonsense, Jamie, nonsense." And I thought so, too.

And then I said, "Grandma, Adam and Eve had two

sons, didn't they? Their names were Cain and Abel."

Grandma, sensing a trap, answered, "Yes, my boy."

"Well, then," I went on, "how come they didn't have any girls. Maybe Cain and Abel wouldn't have gotten into such an argument."

Grandma said that it was a good point and she would ask Mr. Garnett about it. I saw Grandma smile inside and I could tell that she was going to fix him next Sunday, and I felt pretty big.

I was going through some of my things in my room today because it was cold and rainy outside and it was Saturday and there wasn't much of anything going on. One of the things that I found was a paper that I wrote for my Sunday school teacher when I was in sixth grade. My father said at the time that he thought that it was an overripe fruit of religious education. But I kept it in an old shoe box anyway, and I came across it when I was looking for the snapshot of Virginia and me on my sixth birthday.

> King Solomon was a man that lived so many years in the country that he was the big cheese. He was a wise man. One day two women came to him. Each of them was holding the legs of a baby and nearly pulling the kid in two. King Solomon wasn't feeling too good that day because he had been up late to a party the night before, and said why couldn't the kid have been born twins and stop this mix-up over the baby before it started. He called for a sword to split this innocent child so each woman could have one half. Then the real mother of

the baby butts in and says to King Sol., "Stay thy hand your majesty and let the hag have the child, for if I can't have a whole baby I don't want any baby." King Sol. listened to her and then he said, "Take the baby home and wash its bottom," for he knew then that it was her baby and told the other dame to go chase herself. King Sol. was the first mason and built Solomon's temple. He had 700 wives and more than 300 lady friends and that is why there are so many masons in the world. My father said that King Solomon was hot stuff and I think that he was quite a guy myself. The end.

...GOLF, GOPHERS, AND FUNERALS...

MY FATHER BEING A DRUGGIST WAS ONE OF THE BUSINESS men in town who started the Country Club. My mother used to take me out there on Wednesday afternoon. It was called Ladies Day, but most of the ladies just sat all afternoon on the big porch. They were too scared to play golf because of the garter snakes and the spotted adders and sometimes a bull snake that would be out there hunting gophers.

I liked to go to the Country Club because we kids always had grape Blatz pop after lunch. The building had a nice smell of new wood, especially on a hot afternoon when the sun would beat down and make the pine smell come out and the resin drip on the floor and I would get some of it stuck on my bare feet until my mother made me wear my sandals which scratched.

They even had a shower in the locker room and you could take a shower any time. But there wasn't any bathtub and no place to play with a celluloid boat. I had never seen a shower before. I thought everybody took a bath in a tub, but not here at the Country Club. The floor of the locker room was covered with little dents from the nails on the men's shoes which they wore when they played golf so they wouldn't spin around and fall on their behinders when they missed the ball. Sometimes I would go in the locker room and there would be men walking around without any clothes on and showering and drying and scratching and powdering themselves and all laughing and talking and having a good time.

Dickie Drummond and Carolyn Kress and I went out to the Country Club once a week. Dickie and I were still too little to be caddies. I didn't like Dickie Drummond very much because he liked to squash bugs and hurt birds and cut them open when they were still wiggling. Sometimes he would put water in a pail and go around trying to drown gophers. I went with him sometimes. But not often because I like gophers and I don't like to see them get drowned and have their homes flooded. But come to think of it, I never did see a drowned gopher, but I'll bet their houses were a mess after Dickie poured water in the front door.

Dickie would be busy pouring water down a hole. He was so busy that he never saw the gopher come out the back door right behind him and watch him. But Dickie kept trying to drown them. I couldn't ever tell him anything, like the gopher coming out of another hole, for instance.

Those gophers had a hard life. If the bull snakes weren't after them, the crows were. Then once a week they had to watch out for Dickie Drummond and his pail of water. They were busy all the time trying to stay alive. I remember one time when a gopher heard a golf ball go "thunk" on the ground right at his front door and he came up to see what was going on and another man hit another golf ball to the same place and hit the gopher. He did a somersault in the air and got himself killed. Then his family came out and looked him over but ran away when the men came to get their balls. It must have been like being struck by lightning. He never saw the ball that hit him. When this did happen, like the time I am telling about, the gophers would stand up on their hind legs in front of their holes and look around, and then go down in the ground for a little while. Pretty soon they would stick their heads out and peek around carefully before coming outside again. And so it went every day for the gophers.

I never tired of watching the gophers but I sure got tired of the way that Dickie Drummond made life miserable for them. So I would go back to the clubhouse with Carolyn Kress who was fed up with Dickie too. We would ask our mothers for a nickel to buy some pop and then we would sit on the front steps and drink and talk. All that time we could see Dickie way out by the second hole carrying that darned pail and still trying to drown those poor gophers.

"I know what let's do," Carolyn said, "let's go out back of the clubhouse and roll downhill." It sounded good to me, so we did. We rolled down a few times in the high grass and got dizzy and staggered around and pretended that we were walking like Mr. McArdle on his way home from work or Judge Clabhorn on his way to the Courthouse. The next time down the hill I rolled over a lost golf ball. It was still new and shiny but it had grass stain on it so it was easy to lose in the high grass. I put it in my pocket to take home and give to my father who was always losing golf balls, but mostly on the water hole and sometimes across the road to Lowell Park where it would sail into Schirmer's corn field, and he would say "The hell with it," and use another ball.

Then Carolyn said that we should roll down the hill together, which we did. We both lay down and put our arms around each other and started rolling. First I took the golf ball out of my pocket and put it alongside the empty pop bottle so I wouldn't lose it. When we rolled down the hill the next time she bit me in the shoulder and I felt funny anyway and that didn't help, but we rolled down again. This time when we got to the bottom of the hill she was on top when we stopped and I felt something crawling under my back. I rolled over so fast that it threw Carolyn on the ground. Underneath me was a great big brown and yellow snake.

I let out a yell, and Carolyn screamed and the snake went in the other direction. Sure enough, along came Dickie Drummond who wanted to know what's up. When he asked me where the snake went I pointed in the other direction. I didn't want the snake to get hurt. He didn't mean any harm, and I guess that Carolyn and I scared him as much as he scared us and it was a good thing for the snake that he was a snake and could stand some squashing because Carolyn was sort of fat, which made up for me because I wasn't.

I got to thinking that maybe God told the snake to go there so we would stop rolling in the grass, but I don't know. Anyway, I never went rolling down that hill with Carolyn again, or anyone else either. Not even me. Carolyn always tried every Wednesday afternoon, which was Ladies Day, to get me to roll down the hill with her, but I thought maybe I hadn't better, so I never did. God might send a bigger snake next time and how would I explain that to Grandma? Maybe even a poison one. So I went with Dickie Drummond and pretended that I would rather hunt gophers, which I really wouldn't.

After awhile, Carolyn and I would go hunting golf balls, but only where the grass was flat and there weren't any hills. I was a little leery of snakes, and of Carolyn too. So I didn't play with her much except to hunt golf balls. I especially liked to find golf balls that had a little grass stain on them and had been lying in the sun. They smelled delicious and I liked to rub them on my upper lip where the perspiration was. Then I would lick the green stain off, which tasted good but sort of bitter, and then rub the ball against my shirt to make it shiny. Dickie Drummond said that he caught hell from his old lady for doing that because it stained the shirt, but I guess I am neater and more careful and I didn't get stain on my shirt.

The men golfers would give me ten cents for every ball that I found that didn't have a deep cut on it. They told me that they didn't like smiling balls which is what they looked like. Then I would take the money home and buy candy with it for Virginia and me, and Freddie too, if he was around, which I hoped not most of the time when I had candy for Virginia and me. Sometimes Paul would come over, but he was usually some place else because his grandpa ran the feed barn where the horses were kept and Paul had to help his grandpa, especially on funeral days when he wasn't in school, which was most of the summer.

Paul fixed it up with his grandpa one time for me to sit up with one of the hack drivers at a funeral. It was Mr. Hackmore's funeral and it was a big one because he was a politician and a Democrat and had more friends than most anybody but my father, who was a Republican. There were two horses to each hack and four for the hearse that carried Mr. Hackmore and the casket they put him in, which was gray. There were twelve hacks and I got to ride in the next-to-last one. Paul got to ride up front with his grandpa who drove the hearse.

Every funeral went by our house on the way to the cemetery. The day that I rode to the cemetery, because I paid Paul a dime that I got for finding a golf ball and didn't buy candy for Virginia because she was away, I saw my mother and Grandma and Mrs. Dement sitting on the front porch. Mrs. Dement didn't even stop talking while the procession went by. She didn't even turn around but kept swinging and blabbing all the time. But my mother and Grandma saw me. I didn't call out because funerals are supposed to be quiet and sad. When I waved, and my mother and Grandma saw me on the hack alongside my friend Grover, they stood up from their chairs and just stared. I could see my mother's lips move as she was talking to Grandma and I'll bet my mother said, "Did you ever?" And Grandma said that she never did.

We went by real slow as if the horses knew that they were doing a sad job, which they were. They were very proper on the way to the cemetery but coming back they trotted along gaily and talked to each other and were in a hurry to get back to the stable and have some oats. So I had to hang on to the seat pretty tight and couldn't let go to wave at our house as we went by. It was a fine trip and it only cost me ten cents, and Paul bought some candy and we both had a treat, so that was fair enough because Virginia wasn't home.

When I came home I didn't get bawled out or anything. Everybody was quiet and didn't say a thing. My mother stood at the sink peeling potatoes and didn't even say hello. I went out on the front porch where Grandma was but Mrs. Dement had gone home, probably because she was out of breath in spite of her very large lungs. Grandma didn't even look up, but was being very busy darning one of my father's socks. I could tell that they were both upset. I think that was because they knew that many of their friends saw me riding on the driver's seat with Grover on the way to a funeral. If they weren't going to say anything, I wasn't going to say anything either. My father always told me that the fly does not get into the closed mouth. Then sometimes he would say:

There was an old owl who lived in an oak.
The more he heard the less he spoke.
The less he spoke, the more he heard.
Mrs. Dement ain't like that bird.

And then my father would laugh and Grandma would glare at him, but he didn't mind that.

So I went to look up Freddie and tell him all about the ride and how they get the casket in the grave.

That night, as I was going to sleep, I could hear the hoot owl in the cemetery and it sure sounded lonely in there. I could hear all over again the "whump" as the earth was shoveled on to the casket by Dave Suggett who was the gravedigger. There is no other sound like it. I wonder if Mr. Hackmore heard it, but I guess not. The soul has gone to heaven, even if it was a Democrat one, and the soul doesn't have ears any more nor can it wake up in the ground. Except, if the soul goes to hell, where Mrs. Dement said that Mr. Emerson was, it is very hot and windy and noisy, which means that you would have to have ears or how would you know whether it was noisy or not?

I don't really know.

...HOW BIG WAS ABRAHAM'S BOSOM...

This morning when I woke up it was still dark. I had been dreaming that I was in church and Mr. Garnett was praying and I was kneeling down and waiting for the prayer to end and the sermon hymn to begin so that I could have my chocolate cake and the funny papers. When I woke up I could still hear Mr. Garnett praying, and there was a light in the hall. So I got up out of bed and followed the prayer down the hall and there was everybody kneeling around Grandpa's bed and Mr. Garnett standing at the foot of the bed and holding his prayer book and reading from it. My mother and my father and Grandma were kneeling down and had their heads on the bed and there was Grandpa with a sheet over him up to his chin where the prayer book rested in order to hold his jaw shut. He had a penny on each eye and he was very still and I knew that Mr. Staples would be there pretty soon because the Lord had finally called Grandpa home and he wouldn't have to think that he was in Peoria any more and maybe he would find out where Edna was, and maybe who she was too.

Mr. Garnett prayed, "Depart, O Christian soul, out of this world, in the name of God the Father Almighty who created thee. In the name of Jesus Christ who redeemed thee. In the name of the Holy Ghost who sanctifieth thee. May thy rest be this day in peace, and thy dwelling place in the paradise of God."

My mother started moaning and crying and Grandma stopped her and said, "No more blubbering. Your good father, Charles, is at peace and has his mind back now. You are just feeling sorry for yourself when you ought to throw yourself on the mercy of the Lord." Having said that she put her head down on the bed again, and Mr. Garnett went on praying.

"Into thy hands, O merciful Savior, we commend the soul of thy servant, Charles, now departed from the body. Acknowledge, we humbly beseech thee, a sheep of thine own fold, a lamb of thine own flock, a sinner of thine own redeeming. Receive him into the arms of thy mercy, into the blessed rest of everlasting peace, and into the glorious company of the saints in light. Amen."

Then we all got up and went downstairs to the kitchen and Grandma made coffee and we sat around the table not saying very much. Then my father left us with Mr. Garnett who felt as badly as anybody, and he let Mr. Staples in quietly and the two of them went upstairs. I could hear them, and so could Mr. Garnett, because he started talking and reading from the Bible, and when he got through Mr. Staples had gone and my father came back to the dining room and he looked at Mr. Garnett and nodded, and Mr. Garnett looked at my father and nodded. Then he got up and we followed him to the door and he tipped his hat and went home, and I went upstairs to put some clothes on and I looked in Grandpa's room, and he was gone. The prayer book and the pennies were on the night table, and the top sheet was gone too.

Things were pretty quiet around the house most of the day, and I didn't feel like doing much of anything. So Grandma said that I could answer the back door, which

I did often. About noontime people started coming to the back door. Some knocked and some didn't, but women brought bread and pie and cake and soup, and all sorts of things to eat. Mrs. Dement came too, only she didn't talk at all, only when she had to, and she took care of all the food and set the table in the dining room and put out all the plates that we had. Mrs. Garnett hired Mr. Dauntler's smaller dray wagon and brought up wood folding-chairs from the church and a folding table too, because there wasn't enough room in the kitchen or the dining room to hold everything that was given to us.

While all this was going on, Mr. Staples came to the front door and he had a hammer and a nail and he nailed a long piece of purple, gray, and black ribbon to the side of the porch. Grandma said that he was hanging the crepe, and so he was. Then Grover and Paul's grandfather and Mr. Staples and another man went out to the hearse and brought in the casket where they had laid out Grandpa and they brought it into the front parlor and opened it up. Then the flowers started being delivered and pretty soon the parlor looked like Fallstrom's flower store and looked and smelled fine.

That night I went to the train with my father and we met Uncle Charlie who came out for the funeral. He was wiping his eyes and blowing his nose and saying, "Poor Charles. Poor Charles. May God have mercy on his soul." Then he would sniffle, and feeling better now, would start talking to my father about Big Bill Thompson and J. Hamilton Lewis. My father was polite and didn't say anything because there had been a death in the family.

Lots of people came to the house to see Grandpa and

some of them said, "Didn't Mr. Kingsley look nice? Just like he was asleep." And Grandma said that Grandpa wasn't asleep but that he had gone on to a larger life and now he knew who he was and where he was. Which I thought, "Hurray for Grandma." Pretty soon it was time for bed and the family was choosing who was going to take the first turn sitting up with Grandpa and everybody volunteered at the same time, but my father started bossing and everybody took the time he said for them. I asked Grandma why somebody had to sit up all night, and she said that it was the proper thing to do, which I guess is right. But the next day Paul told me that his grandpa told him that somebody had to stay around to keep the cat out of the casket, and that even the neighbors' cats would try to get in the house. Maybe that's so. I don't know, but that's what Paul's grandpa told him and he works for Mr. Staples when he drives the hearse, and he ought to know.

On the day of the funeral, Mr. Staples and his helpers showed up at the house and Mr. Garnett came over too and the family and the helpers stood around while he said a few prayers and then they took the casket and Grandpa and the flowers down to the church where a whole church full of people were waiting, and Mrs. Kent was playing the organ softly. I think it was "Abide with Me," or something like that, which was very pretty and sad. Grandma wanted Mr. Garnett to have the congregation sing "Onward, Christian Soldiers," but he said "No." To my surprise, Grandma didn't give him an argument. But I could tell that Grandma didn't like funerals because they were sad and dreary. I didn't like them either because everybody behaved so heavy and solemn and pious, even the man who ran the Opera House.

Mr. Garnett didn't pray very long. We said a psalm together about lifting our eyes up to the hills. Then we sang the hymn, "Beyond This Land of Whoa," which Grandma wanted and that Mr. Garnett said was all right. Then we went to the cemetery, but I got to ride inside the hack. I saw Paul up front riding the hearse along with his grandpa, so he got to go too.

We didn't stay around for the grave to be filled in. I was relieved because I didn't have to hear the "whump" as the earth was shoveled in. We all went home. That night we put Uncle Charlie on the train back to Chicago. And Mrs. Dement went home, and so did Mr. Garnett. But by the time that we got back to our house all the furniture was back in place and the table and the folding chairs were gone, and most of the food had been eaten and the rest was put away, and everybody felt relieved because Mr. Staples and the Lord had taken Grandpa away. "The Lord giveth and the Lord taketh away," said Grandma.

My father said, "May he rest in peace." And I went upstairs to bed. As I looked out of my window I saw the sliver of the new moon shining and I knew that everything was all right with Grandpa. I wondered who they would get to keep the books down at the City Hall. I bet they don't ever find anyone as good at that as Grandpa, even when he thought he was in Peoria, which he isn't any more, even in his own mind. And that's good.

About a week later I got to thinking about Grandpa again and how he didn't know where he was for over seven years, so I mentioned the subject to Grandma about how I wondered how Grandpa was doing, if anything. She had an answer, and she sat me down, and herself too, in order to tell me what she thought about. Right off she said that it wasn't her idea because she wasn't bright enough, and in any case, it had been invented back in the days when the church was young. The story she told me went like this:

"Now, see here, Jamie. Everybody has three lives to live. Your first life is nine months long, and is spent in the body of your mother. Even grandmothers were like this once. Your second life, where you are now, is three score years and ten, according to the Bible, but it will vary somewhat, depending upon health and heredity and accident and all the chances and changes of this life. Life number three is eternal.

"Life number one is a life spent in total darkness inside the mother. Life number two is half light, half dark. That's us. Life number three is full light. Life number one is unconscious. Life number two is half-conscious. Life number three is full consciousness. Got it, son?"

I nodded yes. Grandma was not to be stopped, so she went on.

"In life number one there isn't any such thing as desire. Your needs are met before you know you have them. In life number two, you have a lot of desires, but you can't do very well on making your wishes come true. Life number three is such that whatever desire you have, there goes with it the ability to fulfill that desire."

I thought, "Boy, that's pretty good. Now what?"

Grandma said, "In life number one there isn't any such thing as love, joy, peace, truth, mercy, justice,

kindness, and all that sort of thing because you don't
need them. In life number two, where we are now, we
know what these things are but they have a way of leak-
ing through our fingers and not being there when we
need them. In life number three these things become a
real and permanent part of you. Believe me, even according to the Bible, there will be plenty of times when
you will need them. But they will be there." She stopped
a minute to see where she was, or at least she made me
feel that way, but I think that she was trying to see how
much farther she could go with a boy. She looked at me
and decided to go on, which made me feel better than I
have for a long time, certainly since Grandpa went on to
life number three.

"Let's pretend that we could remember life number
one. Nobody can, of course, but let's imagine it. Maybe
it would go like this:

> I am an old man. Nine months and three days
> old. I am being crowded out. I'm not wanted
> here any more. All that I have known is slip-
> ping away from me. Life is almost over. I am
> being gathered to my fathers. And at that
> moment in the delivery room the doctor says,
> "Praise be to God, here comes Jamie." But
> Jamie is crying his head off because he thinks
> that he is dying and he is saying goodby to
> life. And so he comes into life number two.
> Then someday Jamie gets old, like his grand-
> ma, and says all over again, "I am an old man.
> Three score years and ten. I am being crowded
> out. I'm not wanted here any more. All that I

have known is slipping away from me. Life is almost over. I am being gathered to my fathers."

In the delivery room of eternity the Lord says, "Praise be, here comes old James." But James, or Jamie, is saying goodby to life, he thinks.

I rolled that around in my head, but Grandma wasn't quite through. "So, you see, son, you are already in eternity because birth and death are the same thing. It simply depends upon which side of the fence you are on at the time. If you're going through it, we call it death. If you witness it, we call it 'birth.' And that's the way it is. So you see, Grandpa is awake and busy, and he isn't confused any more, and that's good. He is in full light, full consciousness, and he can have what he desires and besides that all those things like love, truth, peace, joy, and kindness are a real and permanent part of him. Don't feel sorry for Grandpa. Feel sorry for us. We have a way to go yet, but he's doing and looking down and smiling at the whole business, which at last makes sense."

Then I went to my room and thought awhile as I lay there in the dark.

...BISHOPS, LAYMEN, AND OTHER CLERGY, AFTER PRAYERFUL CONSIDERATION...

Last Sunday the Rev. Mr. Garnett announced that he was resigning as rector of St. Luke's Parish and that, after much thought and prayerful consideration, he had accepted the call to become rector of a parish in Brooklyn, New York. My father said at the supper table the next day that Mr. Garnett had been trying to get out of St. Luke's for the past two years, ever since Mrs. Emerson gave him all of the late Mr. Emerson's long underwear. He also said that the "mene, mene tekel upharsin," which means the handwriting on the wall, had been up ever since Mr. Garnett commented one Sunday morning that Episcopalians knew how to be wicked in honorable ways even better than the Presbyterians and Methodists, which Grandma said was going some around this town. My father also remembered the time that Mr. Garnett said that Episcopalians were too good to enjoy sin and too sinful to enjoy goodness and that they all lived in a no-man's land without the pleasures or joys of either. Grandma laughed and said that she was the one who visited the Misses Eells, and when they asked her what they had missed in the sermon because they were deaf, my grandma shouted it at them and they were offended and put out with Mr. Garnett and cancelled their twenty-five cents a week pledge which each of the rich old maids gave to the church. And that made the vestry mad at Mr. Garnett and at my grandma, too, but that was a waste of time, my father said.

So my father and the vestry went to Chicago to talk with the bishop. They had to find someone to take Mr. Garnett's place. Mr. Brown said that he knew of a man and that his name was Father Taylor, and right away my father said, "Nothing doing with one of those high churchmen." Then he raved on at the supper table one night and ended his tirade by saying, "The Bible says to 'Call no man Father.'" Grandma corrected him when she said, "James, you're wrong about the Bible, as usual. The Bible says, 'Call no man *your* father.' And that's different. Our Lord didn't have clergy in mind when he made that remark." And that was the end of that.

When Mr. Brown mentioned Father Taylor's name to the bishop, the bishop said that he had never heard of him, but if they wanted him then he must be a very godly man. When the vestry came back from Chicago my father told us about all this and added that the bishop was as smooth as mineral oil on a porcelain doorknob, and that the bishop would rather let the vestry name a new pastor, then the bishop wouldn't get blamed for it if things didn't go too well. So we got Father Taylor and my father wasn't too happy about it but he didn't have any other suggestions, so he stopped crabbing and said that if Grandma and her girl friends were happy with the choice then far be it from him to object. I don't know why my father got so upset about it because every Sunday he stands out on the steps most of the time and comes in to take the collection. Grandma says that he is always around when the blessing comes, and it is a good thing because being in the drug business in that town a man needs all the grace he can get.

Grandma said that Mr. Garnett was a living example that a man can live without faith and love, as long as hope hasn't been taken away from him, and that Mr. Garnett prayed long and often for a call somewhere else, and my father said that a man should be careful what he prays for, especially if it was Brooklyn, but too late now.

Finally the day came when Father Taylor moved in and the bishop was coming out on the train to institute him as rector. My father said that he is surprised that the bishop has not been instituted yet but he meant put in an institution. The bishop came out on the Corn King Limited on Saturday night and stayed out at our house in Uncle Charlie's room, only Uncle Charlie didn't come out with the bishop.

My grandma told me that the bishop's name was Sheldon Griswold, and that he came from western Kansas and that he was part Indian. So I was disappointed when he got off the train and didn't have on his Indian suit with the feathers. He didn't look much like an Indian to me except he was very big and solemn but I could tell that underneath he was kind and remembered what it was like to have been a boy once. Grandma said that I have it easy as a boy compared to the bishop, whose Indian mother was murdered by white soldiers when his white father was away. He smoked a big pipe, but not as big as a peace pipe that the chief smoked in the William S. Hart movies.

Because Franklin Finnegan's father was an Irish Catholic who worked at being an Irishman, but didn't do anything about being a Catholic because Franklin's mother was part Jewish and part Protestant, Franklin got to go to church with me and sit with Grandma when the bishop had church the next morning. Grandma packed two pieces of cake and Franklin and I shared the funny papers. But we got interested in what Bishop Griswold had to say. So after we ate the cake we got back in the pew and listened to him. I didn't understand what he said but I got the idea that he knew what he was talking about except when he said something about "Moab is my washpot" and Grandma told me that Moab was a desert so I wondered where he got the water.

Franklin and I liked the clothes the bishop wore. He had a long cloak like a bathrobe without sleeves, and it was gold and white with a pointed hat to match and that made him look even taller. He carried a great big stick with a curved end which Grandma said was a pastoral staff. The bishop wore a nightie underneath which was so thin that I could see through it, but he had on a purple gown like underwear under that but it didn't have sleeves for the legs, but just for the arms. He looked elegant and Grandma and Franklin thought so too.

I asked Grandma why the bishop walked at the end of the procession instead of up front because it seemed to me that the most important person should come first. After church was over, Grandma explained to Franklin and me that the bishop was a shepherd and he carries his shepherd's staff to guide the sheep and they are all ahead of him. Then I asked Grandma, "How did the sheep know where to go if the shepherd was behind them?" Then my father interrupted and said that if the bishop walked ahead of them and led them they would probably all wander off somewhere else, like at St. Luke's Church, and by the time that the procession was over there wouldn't be anybody left in the sanctuary or at the altar except the bishop. And I thought that maybe he was right. But when the service was over, and everybody was marching out, the bishop got out in the front of the line and even walked ahead of Wilson, the boy who carried the cross at eleven o'clock every Sunday except in the summer when nobody did. The bishop carried his stick just like in olden times the Indian chief carried his coup stick with scalps on it, only the bishop didn't have any scalps on his. (My father said that the bishop had a lot of scalps but most of them were bald-headed bankers and lawyers so they didn't make much of a show.) And he said, too, that the bishop had better watch out because he had dealings all the time with lawyers and clergy, and that our Lord could have stayed out of trouble if he had steered clear of lawyers and clergy. Grandma agreed with my father and the bishop, who listened to all this at the dinner table after church. The bishop laughed too, because he knew that it was so, and the two of them got along fine, and Grandma too, whom he called "Nellie" because he had known her for a long time, but she called him "Bishop" and not "Chief Sheldon," which was good.

That night the bishop went back to Chicago on the train, and because Franklin Finnegan lived up that way, we drove him home too, and his father was sitting on the front porch with his long underwear and his trousers on, but his suspenders were hanging down, and he had his shoes off, and his wife was out hoeing the garden and all the younger Finnegans were running through the sprinkler and having a fine time, except Otis who had cut his toe on a piece of glass in the driveway.

...COPS AND ROBBERS AND MR. HAWLEY AND THE NEW JERUSALEM WHICH WAS THE CHURCH UPSTAIRS IN THE DARK....

THE WOMEN OF THE PARISH DECIDED TO HAVE A PARISH dinner to honor the new rector and give everybody a chance to meet him, including Elmer Wilhelm who only came at Christmas and Easter with a lot of others, only everybody kept hoping that Mr. Wilhelm would leave the church a lot of money, which he had plenty of. He had a third wife, too, and that made it difficult, Grandma said.

The day before the parish dinner, Grandma and some of her friends, including Mrs. Emerson and Miss Scanlon and the Misses Eells, and Mrs. Dement, and I don't remember who all, went down to the church basement to give the place a cleaning because it would cost the guild two dollars to have Lincoln Cardwell do it, so ten women did it instead. They all showed up about two o'clock and they all brought dish cloths to tie around their heads so their hair wouldn't get dusty with all the dust and flurry around the place.

Every Monday morning, Mr. Cardwell came down and cleaned the church and the basement. All the gloves and mittens and scarves and umbrellas and rubbers and overshoes that he found he put in the kitchen. Besides, it was already filled with the leftover rummage from the last rummage sale and Miss Cooper had her Sunday school class in there with all that stuff. I know, because I was in her class and we had trouble sometimes getting enough room for everybody to sit down. When we had to write, like about King Solomon, I sat on a stool at the sink and my writing was curvy because of the drain board and sometimes my pencil would go through the paper.

The women of St. Ann's Guild all showed up and they sure made the dust fly, and Mrs. Dement found a hat that she liked so she bought it for fifty cents. Then after awhile she realized that it was the hat that she had given for the spring rummage that hadn't been sold, and she wanted her money back, and Miss Scanlon, the treasurer of the guild, said, "Not on your life, Hattie." And she had to buy her own hat back. Everybody thought it was funny. I did specially because her name was Hattie. Ha ha.

Then the next day, which was Thursday, St. Agnes' Guild women, which was the guild that my mother belonged to, began bringing in food for the big dinner. That night at 6:30 the dinner was served and we boys were nearly starved to death by then, so we crowded to the front of the line in order to get something to eat and Father Taylor said grace, and we started in.

Father Taylor called out in a loud voice, "Girls and ladies and clergy first," and everybody moved in ahead of us and we got served last and that made me mad because I had waited in line for a long time. I didn't think I was going to like Father Taylor if he got himself served before us kids. But that's the way it was, and that's the way it stayed at every parish dinner.

Finally I got to the table and I had ham and potatoes and green beans (which I hate) and cole slaw and apple pie. We boys didn't have any coffee because we weren't old enough. Anyway, I saw Grandma make the coffee that afternoon about four o'clock. She took a big dish cloth and she dumped three cans of coffee into it and tied the opposite ends together and dropped it into the big coffee pot of boiling water. My father said that coffee made saints. But I wasn't that interested. It sounded pretty awful, besides, so we had milk instead.

The old people were still eating and Father Taylor was telling stale jokes, so we boys sneaked upstairs to the church, and did we have a good time! We didn't turn on the lights up in the church but let the light from the street light be enough. It showed through the stained-glass windows real spooky-like, but we didn't mind that. The guild had just made some new individual kneelers. They got carpet scraps from the Keyes-Ahrens furniture store. They went to Ole Selgestad's saw mill and he gave them a lot of sawdust and they sewed the carpet up like a box and put the sawdust in and they were ready for praying, as my father said.

We boys would hide under the pews and crawl back and forth carrying one of those new hassocks. Then when we would see a shadow, or a shadow that we thought was somebody, we would throw it at him in the dark. I had gotten away from the fellows and got clear down toward the back of the church and then I stood up straight in a shadow so nobody could see me. All of a sudden there was a solid shadow close by and I let fire with my hassock and I caught Mr. Hawley, the Sunday school superintendent, right in the neck when he didn't expect it. He gargled and coughed and stepped backward in order to absorb the shock and then he cried out, "Boys! Boys! This is God's house."

The race was on, and we headed for the back stairs through the sacristy and down to the kitchen and left Mr. Hawley up there in the dark with God. I was kind of red and out of breath when I got to the kitchen and Mrs. Emerson gave me another piece of pie. She did for the rest of the fellows when they showed up too. We had a great time at parish dinners, and I'm not fooling. When I got home I threw up because I ate so much and ran so hard, but it was worth it anyway, because I felt fine again after I got through.

The next Sunday, Father Taylor fixed us by making us feel terrible. At the Sunday school service he asked us first what stained-glass windows did and nobody knew. Then he asked us who those people were whose pictures were in them, and we didn't know that either. Except that I used to think that the window in the back of the church was a picture of God when he was old and the one over the altar was when he was young. That was when I was little, but now I know better, but I didn't know the answers to Father Taylor's questions. Nobody else did either, so he had to tell us.

"Boys and girls," he said, when he finally got collected, "those are the pictures of the twelve apostles. Notice that some were older men and some were younger men. Some had beards and some of them didn't. What did they have in common?"

Francis King said, "Sandals."

Father Taylor looked at the windows and saw that he was right, but that wasn't the answer. So he waited and didn't say anything, so I tried next. "They are all wearing red robes," I volunteered. And so they were, but that wasn't the answer.

Finally Father Taylor gave up and gave us the answer. "Boys and girls," he announced, "those are the men that the Light shines through." I had never thought of it that way, and I don't think that very many of the kids got it, but I did and I think Father Taylor was pretty smart to think of it that way because the light sure did.

I told my father about it at dinner on Sunday after church, and he said, "Yeah, but where would they be if they got the lead out?" And I didn't get it, and Grandma told him that he ought to be ashamed of himself, but he wasn't.

...HER KISS KNOCKED ME DOWN THE STAIRS...

I mowed Mr. Reed's lawn on the hottest day of the year, and I was sweat all over. The only reason that I did it was because I needed the money. There was going to be an ice cream social that night and I had to have some cash. Mr. Reed, who fought in the Civil War and was "full of years," as Grandma said, paid me twenty-five cents. Then I could go to the ice cream social. I was impatient to go and was ready about six o'clock in the evening. But it didn't start until about eight, as soon as it got dark out, because they had the lawn at the church all strung up with Japanese lanterns and it sure looked pretty, but it was hot as sin. It was a good thing that the rectory was right next door, because it made it sort of handy, having a bathroom which everybody could use, which I did.

The fireflies were out and so were the crickets and the night creatures peeping and squeaking. So was the moon, and it was a full moon, colored orange and hung in the sky just over the roof top of Dr. Clevidence's house, who was a dentist, only he was at the ice cream social, too, and wasn't pulling teeth. Dr. Clevidence didn't like the heat, his wife said. So he went through a can of talcum powder every week and always looked white, like a Dracula movie, but he was pink underneath because I saw him that way at the Country Club once, and he was pink all over but under his palm beach trousers and his ponjee shirt. Anyway, it was a beautiful night.

I had been busy all summer doing a number of things and I had almost forgotten about Virginia. But there she was carrying trays of ice cream and ice water. Something had happened to her since school was out. She no longer walked. She floated across the lawn. She was radiant, and I almost went to pieces when I saw her. All the old signs appeared: the dry throat; the inability to say anything. My forehead got awfully hot, and I felt like a dud. I dropped my spoon on the grass and when I leaned over to pick it up I stepped on my hand. Her beauty sure did me in.

First, she brought me a glass of water and said, "Hello, Jamie," and she smiled, and I got slack-jawed. Then she brought me a big dish of homemade ice cream with home-grown strawberries on top of it, and another glass of water. Then she held out her hand for my nickel, and I dropped it in the grass before I could get it to her hand I was shaking so much. We both got down to look for the nickel and we bumped heads and I thought I would faint. Finally, she found the nickel and went away to wait on Dr. Clevidence and Elmer Wilhelm, and I don't know who all. So I ate my ice cream.

I was sitting with Freddie and Franklin Finnegan and they had some more money, like I did, so they ordered some more ice cream from Virginia and I couldn't do anything but nod. So I had some more ice cream and another glass of water.

Well, just to shorten things up, I had five dishes of homemade ice cream and home-grown strawberries and eleven glasses of water. They were all brought to me by

Virginia and I thought that this was paradise. But I had
to go, and quick, so I went over to the rectory, which
made it kind of handy. I thought that I would be there a
week before I finished, but pretty soon I came back and
the ice cream social was breaking up. Virginia was all
through working and was getting ready to go home. She
saw me and said, "C'mon, Jamie, let's go home." That
was fine, but I could barely walk I was so nervous.

There were seven long blocks to walk and I could
never seem to get in step with Virginia. First I would be
on the edge of the sidewalk and the next step I would
bang her shoulder. I even missed the curb at Henry
Noble's corner, and I had a very embarrassing time. The
closer we got to Virginia's house the more nervous I became until I was almost in a panic. Whatever I said
sounded stupid. Whenever I walked I had two left feet.
Either she didn't notice my suffering or she was such a
young lady that she tried not to notice. It was all I could
do to walk up the seven steps to her front porch. Then
what was I going to do?

Like a dope I just stood there alongside the screen
door. I said, "Thank you for a wovely weavening."

Virginia said, "Thank you, Jamie. It was a lot of fun."

Then I picked my nose a moment and said, "Well,
good night."

Virginia said, "Good night, Jamie." It sounded like
music from a heavenly harp, but still I stood there like
a dope and couldn't move except to try to get my feet
on straight. Then Virginia turned and said, "I must go
inside, now." She had one hand on the screen door
handle and I was holding on to the porch railing as if
I were clinging to a sinking ship. She reached over and

kissed me on the cheek and then went in the house real fast.

That kiss burned clear through to my teeth and I remembered the time that she kissed me there when I was a little boy hanging upside down in a cherry tree. I pledged my life to her. And she was so beautiful. Then I collected myself and turned and started down the steps, but I missed the first step and fell all the way to the bottom and I made an awful racket and lit square on my behinder on the cement walk. That reminded me right away that even though the rectory wasn't next door, which would have been sort of handy, I wasn't going to make it all the way home. I didn't even see how I was going to stand up in that condition. I did manage to do it, but I stumbled over to the nearest maple tree, and on the shady side of the tree, that is, away from the street light, I just had to let go. While I was standing there collecting myself and beginning to feel better I looked back at the house and there in the upstairs hall window I could see Virginia looking out at me. Real fast I started walking so that she wouldn't know what was going on and I messed myself up and when I got home had to go in the back door and up the back stairs so that Grandma wouldn't see what had happened to me.

Oh, Virginia, why do I fall apart when I look at you? Why can't I tell you how wonderful you are? It would be quite enough even to worship and adore you at a silent distance. At least I can love you secretly and no one will know. How can I ever face you again after you saw me doing what I was doing in your front yard?

Do you think that you can ever forget what a dope I am?

Virginia, I love you.

...FATHER TAYLOR, FATHER FOLEY, AND FIRPO, AND A COUPLE OF PREACHERS WHO DIDN'T KNOW WHAT THEY WERE GETTING MIXED UP WITH...

MY FATHER CALLED FATHER TAYLOR "THE WILD BULL of the Pampas." This meant that my father was reminded of Angel Luis Firpo who had a prize fight with Jack Dempsey, only Jack knocked Firpo clear back to the fourth row in the fourth round, which must have meant something to Firpo like wishing he was somewhere else, my father said. Sometimes he would call Father Taylor "Father Firpo" when he wasn't around. He didn't call him that because he was big, because Father Taylor was more like a banty rooster, but because he was always getting into situations that he should not get into because he didn't know how to handle them when he got there, so all he ever did was put his head down and swing. Or so my father said at the supper table one night. Father Taylor always made matters worse because he didn't mince words and everybody knew where he stood before he started telling everybody where he stood.

And as my father said, "That isn't very good around this town." And I guess it wasn't because he's been around it long enough to know what he's talking about.

My father also said that some day one of the influential Dempseys around this town would knock him clear back to the foot of the lake at Fond du Lac, Wisconsin, where he came from and he wouldn't even have time to grab his three-cornered funeral hat which Miss Eustace said through her mustache made him look like an Irish Catholic and had everybody confused and the Irishmen thought that Father Foley up at Holy Mother Mary Mystical Rose of Perpetual Help Church had another new assistant. Father Foley did have a new assistant about every six months, so it was confusing. My father also said that both Father Foley and Father Taylor had it coming to them; Father Taylor because he was always upsetting community applecarts, and Father Foley because he was always feuding with the Italian curates that Bishop Fenstermacher sent to him to break in. My father also said that the bishop was really trying to break up Father Foley but Father Foley didn't look as if anybody would ever break him up. And I guess nobody ever did.

Besides that, the Methodists started complaining to my father about Father Taylor, and the Presbyterians lined up right behind them. All this was mainly because he and Father Foley were on such good terms. I think that they both needed friends, which made it nice that they were both around to hold each other up when things got sticky, which they did pretty often here in Euphor City.

I knew from the Murphy twins and Jerome Keenan and Ovid O'Malley that Father Foley scolded the congregation nearly every Sunday for drinking bootleg whiskey

made by a Lutheran bootlegger, who was Jake Schirmer.
I know who made it because I overheard a conversation
one day down at the drug store between my father and
Chief of Police Vann Bipper, who came in the store for
some corn plasters. They didn't know that I was on the
other side of the counter all bent over putting away some
hot water bottles that had just come in. Chief Bipper and
my father got to laughing about it because they were
good friends.

There is a story about why they are good friends. My
father makes the gin mix in the prescription room and
sells it for fifty cents for eight ounces. I watched my
father and Dewey make the stuff. First you put two
ounces of something called glycerin in the bottle, then
you add from an eye-dropper three drops of juniper
juice and fill the bottle up with distilled water. Then the
buyer goes down the street to Vaile's pool hall to hunt up
Jake Schirmer and get the alcohol to put in with it and
make the gin. This costs two dollars for eight ounces
which was called a "weasel." My father's end of the deal
was legal but the Methodists wouldn't trade at my
father's drug store because he was helping John Barley-
corn, whoever he was. I've never seen him, even at the
pool hall. However, when a man would get caught with a
bottle of gin mix that had the alcohol mixed in because
he had already seen Jake, then the police would arrest
him if they found out about it because that was the law.
Then the police would take the bottle and use it in court
as evidence. Judge Clabhorn, running his tongue over
his lips real slow, would ask how did the officer know
there was alcohol in the bottle. The police couldn't prove
it until the bottle was taken down to my father's store

and sometimes he would test it with a funny looking tube to see for sure if there was any alcohol in it. I never did find out how my father knew, but I did know that he did and he would tell the police and the police would tell the judge and the victim would get fined and my father would be paid five dollars for his work and besides that he always got the bottle back and was still in business. I knew more of what was going on around there than my father thought because I had Dewey around to explain things. Dewey also told me that he was named Dewey because his father was on Admiral Dewey's flagship in the Spanish-American War, and that if Dewey had been a girl he would have been named "Olympia" after the battleship. It's a good thing Dewey was a boy. I wondered sometimes what Dewey's mother would have done to his father if Dewey had been a girl and was named after a battleship.

I told my grandma what I heard between Chief Vann Bipper and my father and about Father Foley and Jake Schirmer. She kept looking into her darning basket as though she was trying to find something and then she said while she went on rummaging among the socks and threads and needles, "I don't see why the Irish Catholics pick on the Lutherans. Nearly everybody knows that the pope in those days must not have been very bright because if he had been bright he would have known that the only trouble with Martin Luther was that he wanted to be a bishop and the Italians didn't catch on and so it started the whole mess and even to this day German bishops send Italian curates to Irish pastors." I remembered what she said because I wanted to understand it someday but I don't suppose I ever will. Grandma sounded very sure of what she was saying, as she usually does, and is right most of the time. Certainly as far as I'm concerned.

Things got going hot and heavy around town and all the issues were tangled up and everybody bawling out everybody else and blaming the other person for his troubles. When the Methodists found out that they couldn't get anywhere by picking on Father Foley and started in on Father Taylor, they started in on my father, too, and that wasn't very bright.

"This is a waste of time," he said to the whole family at the supper table. "I can hold my ground and not lose a single customer in this town. They all go to the Rexall store in the first place."

Grandma tried to explain what it was all about. I was twelve going on thirteen, now, so I could pick things up faster than when I was five. "Jamie," she said, "a few years ago Mr. Reed used to have a grocery store on Galena Avenue. He got old and sold his business and the buyer moved all the groceries down to a building that he owned on Hennepin Avenue and the store was empty. Mr. Reed thought it over for awhile and then decided to give the building to St. Luke's Church. He was on the vestry when you were a little boy. He didn't need the money or the building but the church did, so he gave the property to the parish.

"Well, the vestry finally found someone to rent the building to, after almost a year went by. They rented the first floor to Mr. Vaile for his billiard parlor, whom you know because I've seen you come out of there and Mr. Vaile chasing you as far as the alley because you are too young for pool halls, I know." She stopped for a minute to give that news a chance to sink in so that I wouldn't get the idea that I was getting old enough to outsmart Grandma, and besides that she was looking around for a sock that she hadn't darned yet. She went on, as she put her darning egg in a brown sock of my father's. "You know that Mr. Vaile is an Irish Catholic, and he always pays his rent on time and keeps the building clean and runs a good place, considering that it's a disgrace to the town because it's a pool hall."

I interrupted. "Yeah, I know, Grandma. There's never a fight inside. Mr. Vaile makes them go out in the alley. And that's where Jake Schirmer does his bootlegging, except when he comes inside in the winter to get warm."

Grandma looked at me as though it reminded her of something. But whatever it was, she thought better of it and said, "Getting pretty smart for your britches, aren't you, son?" I agreed with her.

She had some more to say so she said it. "Bootlegging is against the law and that's good. But it is a poor law, and that's bad. Then too, Jake is all crippled up and has a wife and five children to feed and his mother who is the children's grandma, and it is the best he can do."

I happen to know why Jake is all crippled up and Grandma doesn't, and I am going to leave it there as far as she is concerned. About a year ago the police were after Jake and he was running down the alley to get away from them. He came to the railing that went around the outside entrance to the Bee Hive Department Store. Either he forgot how far down it was on the other side, or else he didn't think about it at all, which is most likely. Anyway, in his big hurry he hurdled the rail for some dumb reason and fell fourteen feet carrying an armful of bottles full of alcohol. All the bottles broke, as did Mr. Schirmer's ankles, so they didn't have any evidence against him, but he was laid up for a long time because he was also all cut up. My father said that Jake didn't need any antiseptic because he was up to his knees in hundred-proof potato alcohol anyway.

The Methodists and Presbyterians were trying to get my father and the vestry to be tough landlords and throw Mr. Vaile out of the place because Jake used the pool hall to get warm in and to contact customers. When nobody paid any attention to that then they started in again because the second floor was rented out as the Labor Temple. They said that the Episcopal church was in cahoots with the Socialists on the one hand and the Democrats and the Irish Catholics on the other.

That made my father angry. Real mad. Not a nosy, hot mad, like a mackerel snatcher, but a cold mad. And boy, was he chilly! He wasn't angry because they hinted that he wasn't a good Republican to let all that stuff go on in a church-owned building, because he didn't think that it was any of their nosy business in the first place. Besides, my father knew that one of their church pillars owned a house that kept girls for parties on Saturday nights down on the west side. My father even said at the supper table that the pillar in question also owned the business but nobody really knew—which is good, I guess. When my father reminded them about it he didn't hear any more from that Reverend and the group that came to see him. Then he got it from some other people and my father didn't spare the horses on them. He turned to this other preacher who was their spokesman and right front of them he said to that Reverend,

"Your wife has been shoplifting here for over two years and I've never said or done anything about it up until now. I figure that as of now she owes me fifty-seven dollars and forty-three cents and I've never sent you a bill. Now, what is it you want me to do for you?"

I wish that I had been there to see the looks on the faces, but I missed it. I knew something else about it that I guess my father knew too. And that is that the preacher's brother-in-law, Harvey, who lives with them got caught by Vann Bipper one night sitting in a tree outside Mitzie Miller's bedroom and got let off the first time. My father was too decent a man to mention it even if he did know about it. All us kids knew. I found out later that when he got caught the second time that he got himself locked up for his troubles. When Judge Clabhorn asked him how long he had been doing this ol' Harvey told the judge that there wasn't a woman in town that he hadn't seen nekkid. I bet the judge licked his lips like he did when he asked about the booze.

And Father Taylor probably knew about all these things too. I'll bet that Father Foley did too. I think everybody in town was getting pretty nervous and uncomfortable with them knowing so much about what went on, and my father too, running the drug store and all. And then what Grandma knew besides, because she told me that she had lived in Euphor City for seventy-six years, and you can't be around town that long without learning a lot that maybe you shouldn't and wouldn't do you much good if you did. One day Father Taylor asked Grandma if she had lived there all her life, and she said, "Not yet, hardly. I have a few more years yet." And so she did.

...LINCOLN CARDWELL'S SATURDAY MIRACLE...

IT WAS ABOUT THIS TIME THAT FATHER TAYLOR STARTED Confirmation classes on Saturday morning down in the basement of the church. Grandma decided that it was time that I was prepared for Confirmation, and then be confirmed when the bishop came out in the spring to visit the parish. He always came out on the Corn King Limited and went home on Sunday night on the Clinton Passenger, which left about five o'clock, when it was on time, which was about twice a week, but never on Sunday.

I was all keen for going to Confirmation class because the girls would be there and we would have fun. Then I found out that there would be old people there, too, like Lincoln Cardwell, the colored sexton, and his wife, Juanita, which was fine but they were older. Grandma said that the Episcopal church was the only church that didn't get upset when they came to service, except up at St. Patrick's, but that Lincoln and Juanita weren't Irish enough for the Donovans and the Shaughnessys. So they were going to be in the class with us and then clean the church for Sunday. I figured they wouldn't bother us kids. They never had any of their own, but they liked kids and they were kindly people.

I remember once when I was down at the church on Saturday to deliver the flowers for Sunday in memory of Grandpa, and Mr. Cardwell was having trouble with the furnace because the grates broke. He worked a long time wiring them together so they would last through the winter. Then he asked me to help him put them in by holding the other end. Before we did, Mr. Cardwell told me that twice the wire slipped and he had to take them out and wire them together again. So this was the third time and he had put them together best of all. But he said, "Jamie, I don't know if this will work or not so I'm gonna pray first." Then he got down on his knees in all the ashes, and he said real loud, with his eyes closed and his head up, "Lord, show thy power." And then we put the grates back in and they stayed! Mr. Cardwell had an expression on his face that gave me the idea that he knew they would all the time, and the only reason that he hadn't prayed the first two times was because he didn't want to bother the Lord on a Saturday morning when he was getting ready to take Sunday off.

So I went to the first class, and everybody was there. All eight of us, including the Cardwells. Father Taylor started explaining that we would meet together every Saturday from January eighth until after the first of May, when the bishop came. He also said that by the time that we were coming near the end of our instruction we would already be prepared to make our confessions.

That did it. No more Confirmation instruction for me. I wasn't going to get mixed up in that Irish Catholic business. So I talked to Grandma about it.

She thought it over awhile and finally said, "Jamie, Father Taylor is *almost* right. It won't hurt you any, and now that you are going into adolescence the more things that you get going your way then the easier it will be."

"Did you ever make your confession, Grandma?" I asked.

"Of course not!" she fired back. "What does that have to do with it?"

"What's good for kids is good for grandmas," I said, feeling pretty smart. The next thing I knew I got a swat alongside the head. Then next Saturday I went back to Confirmation class.

Sometimes Father Taylor would let us out early and then I would go sliding with Virginia and a whole gang of kids, including David Mandelbaum from Ulm, whose folks were visiting the Steins who owned the Bee Hive Department Store. There was lots of snow and everybody went out to Miles Hill on the edge of town. The sliding was good enough to take you all the way down to the ice house if you didn't drag your feet crossing Artesian Road, which I did sometimes.

My first time down Miles Hill I slammed down, which means to run with your sled and then drop it and fall on it fast so you get a good start. I hit the curb hard at Artesian and broke a runner on my sled. I was looking it over and feeling sorry for myself when Virginia went by, but she dragged her feet so she wasn't going too fast to make the corner. She went almost all the way to the ice house and then started pulling her sled up the hill. When she got up to where I was and saw what had happened, she asked me to slide with her. Virginia had a new Flexible Flyer sled which bends in front and steers best and can do all the corners fast and stay right-side-up.

When we got to the top of the hill and pointed the sled downhill, Virginia would lie on her stomach and steer. I would put my hands on the back of her legs and run hard in order to give us a good start and then I would kneel on the space on the back of the sled and hunch down and put my hands on the steering gear alongside hers and away we would go. But we had our mittens on. I would put my head down out of the wind right up against her cheek, and that was great. We laughed and cheered and had such a good time that I wanted to slide with her the rest of my life.

But that wasn't all, because when anybody was sliding down the hill and went by the Irish kids coming up the hill they would throw snowballs and yell out, "N'y-a-a-, ya dirty Protestant," and plug you with a snowball. When they saw me coming with Virginia they called us both dirty Protestants and called me a sissy. But I just lay lightly on top of Virginia, paying them no mind, or at least only enough to duck snowballs. I didn't get hit once and that's pretty lucky for an Episcopalian. Besides it gave me an excuse to be close to Virginia.

After we made the run Virginia would sit on the sled and I would pull her up the hill until I started slipping on the steep part, then she would get off and take the rope with me and we would pull the sled to the top of the hill again. Except we would stop and pull over to the side when any of the Irish kids went by, which seemed to be most of the time. I would make snowballs and have them ready. I hit Jerome Keenan right in the eye and he didn't make the turn at Artesian and he smashed into the curb like I did, only he didn't break his sled. The Murphy twins were right behind him and they piled up too. All three were hopping mad and called me a lot of nasty words and bragged about what they would do to me if Virginia wasn't there to see the mess that they would make of me. But they never did.

The next time that Virginia and I went down the hill we sat on the sled. I would sit behind her and hold my arms around her waist and she would hold on to my arms and stick her feet straight out in front so that my feet could steer the sled. The trouble with sliding this way was that it was too easy for somebody coming up the hill to get a hold of you and spin you around and turn you over. I liked lying down best for a couple of reasons. One of them was that it was harder for the roughnecks to grab you as you went by.

I slid with Virginia and the rest of the gang until almost dark, then we went to her house and Paul and Freddie and Carolyn came along, too, and "Heavy Eva" Morse who invited herself when she heard that there was going to be hot chocolate. Virginia was too polite to say she couldn't come. Then we had hot chocolate and cookies and we all went home. But we went sliding again that night after supper. There weren't very many Irish kids out after supper on Saturday because they all had to go to Father Foley's church and tell him how bad they were in a closet in the back of the church. We Protestants could slide until nine o'clock, and that beats being a mackerel snatcher, which was what Freddie called the Irish kids.

...HOW IT HAPPENED TO ADAM, AND HOW IT ALL GOT STARTED...

It got closer and closer to the time for the bishop to come for Confirmation and I learned quite a lot about many things, and got answers to some questions that had been bothering me. Like what the church was all about. Father Taylor said that everywhere one went there were two congregations in every parish. At first I didn't understand what he meant, then he explained. He said that in every congregation there was a small number of people who knew what the gospel was, and what the faith and practice of the church was. But there was a larger number of those in the parish who didn't have much of an idea about those things. He said that they believed all sorts of superstitious things which they put in place of the Christian religion because they didn't like too much what the Lord told them to do and they had some better ideas, like Adam did. I didn't get all that the first time, but then Father Taylor told us a story. As I remember it, the story went like this.

One day the Lord became tired of being alone and he decided to make the earth. He was busy for a long time making oceans and lakes and rivers and creeks and mountains and valleys. He also spent much time making fish, reptiles, birds, and mammals. One day when he was making the first camel, and things weren't going too well, he sat down on a log to rest, and it occurred to him that he was bored with the whole thing. He thought and thought for a long time.

Finally, he got a bright idea, and said to himself out loud, "I know what I'll do. I'll make a man!" And in a flash, there was the first man sitting on the other end of the log. He turned to the man and said, "Good morning. Your name is Adam. I'm the Lord."

Adam sat there and looked at the Lord, and the Lord looked at Adam and the Lord thought that he had done a good job for his first try at making any creature as complicated as Adam. Then the Lord said, "Adam, how do you like all the things that I have made? See the grass, the trees, the river, and the hills? I made all those."

But Adam didn't have anything to say. He just looked it all over, including a chipmunk that scrambled up on the log. So the Lord went on with his talking, "You know, Adam, I get tired making these things alone. It isn't any fun. So I started thinking again and I decided to make a man like you. Then I would have somebody to help me finish creation and we could have a dandy time making things."

The Lord was getting warmed up now, so he went ahead and explained some things to Adam about who he was, that is, who *Adam* was. "I have given you four things that you will need if you are going to share with me in the finishing of creation. I haven't given these four things to any other creature. Just you." And Adam looked at the Lord and wondered what those things were, so the Lord told him.

"The first gift is the gift of reason. I have given you the ability to solve problems. I have even given you the ability to create problems to solve. I can do those things and I created you and I think sometimes that when I created you I created a problem to solve. But, anyway, I have already done it. I am giving you the ability to make choices and to plan ahead and make appointments, and break them too, if you like. Besides that I give you the ability to make things that you don't need, just for the fun of inventing and creating."

And Adam just looked straight ahead and took it all in. The Lord ended by saying that there was one more gift and that was the ability to give one's life for somebody you didn't like, the same as the Lord did on Good Friday. When the Lord had finished explaining all those things he ended by saying, "That's what the Bible means when it says that man was made in the image of God."

Adam got up off the log and walked back and forth, using his mind for the first time, and that made him in God's image. And he started planning, and that made him in God's image too. Next, Adam started clearing away the underbrush and making a place for a picnic and he made a mattress of pine boughs, so he started creating things. But the last gift that made him in God's image puzzled Adam and he wasn't so sure that he wanted that one. But anyway, he thought it over. Finally he clapped his hands together, and he smiled, and he turned to the Lord and said, "Lord, I think your idea is great. I have some great plans already on how to finish the world, so I tell you what *you* do. Why not go up on the moon and get that going? In the meantime I'll get some committees organized and have things going here by Monday, and when you get back you won't recognize the place."

The Lord was disappointed because Adam wanted to do it all by himself. Father Taylor called it "Original Sin." I thought that it was original too, and besides, now I understood why the world isn't finished yet.

When I went home I told Grandma all about that story. She said that it didn't read like that in the Bible and what was Father Taylor trying to do by getting all these strange ideas in children's heads. And that was the end of it.

Then the last class before the bishop came, Father Taylor explained to us how to make our Communion. He said that we should all come to the early service at eight o'clock on Sunday and make our Communion and then come back at eleven and be confirmed by the bishop. He also said that our Communion would be better if we didn't eat breakfast before we came to church. Then he went on to tell us about Confirmation and said that when the bishop laid his hands on our heads we would receive the gifts of the Holy Spirit, and he explained what they were, and that we would never be the same again.

So on Sunday morning I was curious and excited when I started off to church. I set my own alarm and I was quiet so that I wouldn't wake up my mother and my father and Grandma. But Grandma was already up and had my breakfast ready, but I said I would make a fasting communion and have breakfast when I came back from church. For once, Grandma didn't have much to say, but let me go my own way.

I became sort of dizzy and woozy at church but I pulled myself together enough to go to the altar rail and kneel down. I was sort of disappointed, though, because the bread tasted like fish food and the wine tasted funny. And then all of a sudden nothing at all happened, although I waited. I could not understand it because I had made my preparation the night before as I was instructed. I sort of got the idea that it was going to be a big thing, but I remember that Father Taylor said that sometimes it takes awhile for it to work. All the way home I waited for something to happen, but it never did.

Then I went back to church at eleven o'clock and went up to kneel in front of the bishop for the laying on of hands, while he said at the same time, "Defend, O Lord, this thy child, that he may continue thine forever and daily increase in thy holy Spirit more and more until he come into thy heavenly kingdom." The bishop's breath whistled through his nose as he got ready for the next person, who was Virginia. And nothing happened then, either, which of course made me think it was me. All I felt was his heavy hands on my head. I didn't say anything about these things to anybody, including Grandma, because I thought that probably it was all my fault because nothing happened.

I kept on trying for several weeks and then didn't pay much attention to the business, except when I took my turn serving at the altar, which was on the first and third Sundays at eleven o'clock and at eight o'clock on the second and fourth Sundays, when I served with Greenie Edson who never came to the late service to help John Crabtree and me.

One time we were complaining about serving at eleven o'clock church and John and I felt that Father Taylor was taking advantage of us, so I said to John that I would light the candles on the altar then I would sneak out and join him at Fulf's Confectionery Store. I caught up with him on the way over, and we were sitting there reading the funny papers, and I looked down and saw a pair of polished black shoes and what looked like the bottom of a cassock. I lowered the paper and there was Father Taylor.

He didn't scold us or anything, but said, "Come on, boys, follow me." And we did, and we rode back to church in his Ford and we served him that day too, and he never said a thing about it, ever. But I remember the opening hymn and it made John and me laugh whenever we heard it because it was:

> As of old, Saint Andrew heard it
> By the Galilean lake,
> Turned from home and toil and kindred,
> Leaving all for his dear sake.

Father Taylor's first name was Andrew.

...NO MORE LAND OF WHOA FOR GRANDMA, LOOK, LORD, HERE SHE COMES!...

THERE WAS A TERRIBLE THUNDER AND LIGHTNING STORM last night. It woke me up out of a sound sleep. I lay there listening to the wind blow and the rain beat on the tin roof over my bedroom. Then I saw a sliver of light under Grandma's door. In a moment she came groping her way down the hall to the bathroom and she hit her nose again, as she always did so consistently, but especially I remember the times that she did when she came to my room in a storm to comfort me. But those days are gone and she no longer can hold me in her arms, nor does she need to, because I am really beginning to grow up.

I lay in bed quietly and waited for Grandma to go back to her room. Finally she did. First she called to me.

"Jamie," she said hoarsely, "will you help me to my room?"

This was the first time that Grandma ever asked anybody to help her. I got up out of bed and went to her and put my arm around her waist and led her to her bed. I asked if I should call my mother or my father and she shook her head. I got her into her bed and she heaved a big sigh and I was about to turn out the light and say goodnight when she said, "Pull up Grandpa's rocker, Jamie. I want to talk to you. There isn't much time left."

I reached over and slid the rocking chair up close to the bed, wondering what was on her mind. Then she began.

"My grandson, I think that I am going to leave you tonight, and go like your grandfather did. He used to try to tell me how it felt, and now I think I know."

I tried to be light about it, thinking maybe it was just the oppressive heat and the storm, but she interrupted me.

"Now listen to what I have to say, my boy. I have been having flashes of lightning, just like your grandfather told me that he had. That is followed by a thunderclap inside my head and I seem to light up and then everything grows quiet. I think that there is a last big one coming soon. Maybe next week. Maybe tomorrow. Maybe tonight. It doesn't really matter much. I have led a good life, and I have had you with me for more years than I deserve."

There was a silence while she looked at the ceiling, and I started looking at the floor. I suggested that I call my mother and my father again. Grandma said, "Sit and be still, Jamie. It's you I want to talk to." She shifted around and held her forehead for a moment. "When I go, Jamie, I want the service to be as short and painless as possible. Tell Father Taylor that I want the hymn that you always called, 'Beyond this Land of Whoa.' There is no use in asking him to use 'Onward, Christian Soldiers,' or, as you used to say, 'Conrad's Sister's Shoulders.' The church isn't up to it yet. It was once and it will be again, but not for me, so don't insist on that one. And another thing, Jamie, I don't want any tottering old men carrying me to my final resting place. I want Freddie and Franklin and Paul and you, and whoever else you want, like maybe Dan McArdle and Lincoln Cardwell. But don't let anybody talk you out of it." Then she asked me for a glass of water, and I went to the bathroom and got it for her. When I came back I lifted her head and helped her take a sip.

"Jamie," she said, "I lived long enough to see you confirmed and growing up into a fine young man. I have only a thimble full of time left, but it is enough. . . . Goodby, Jamie. I'll see you later. Here it comes!"

Grandma stiffened like an electric shock had gone through her, then she lay still. I didn't have to touch her or feel her pulse. I just knew. It was proper that Grandma should die in a thunderstorm and with lightning flashing and all nature in an uproar. Without hardly thinking, I reached over to the night table and took the prayer book and put it under her chin so that her mouth and lips would stay closed. Then I went back to my room and found two pennies on my dresser top and put them on her closed eyes. Then I woke up my mother and my father and they came rushing into Grandma's room.

My mother said, "Did you ever?"

And Grandma couldn't give the answer of the years, so for her I said, "No, I never did."

Mother turned to me and stared, then she burst into tears and my father and I had quite a time with her. I hadn't realized, really, until this thunderous night how much she depended upon Grandma for everything. The next day I realized that everybody always did. Instead of calling Father Taylor I said the prayers myself from my own prayer book. Grandma would have liked that. After that, my father called the doctor and Mr. Staples, and that was that, except that I told my father and my mother about the talk Grandma and I had, and they agreed, which relieved me, because I thought that maybe they would think that I dreamed it all up.

Grandma was very much at her own funeral. Everybody felt deeply that a whole age was passing. To me it was like watching a person stand on the back platform of a train as it approached the vanishing point into the curve of eternity, and Grandma was on it, and going first class to the destination that she never had the slightest doubt about.

> There is a blessèd home,
> Beyond this Land of Whoa,
> Where trials never come,
> Nor tears or sorrows flow;
>
> . . . .
>
> Wait but a little while,
> In uncomplaining love!
> His own most gracious smile,
> Shall welcome you above.

Grandma was sure about many things. That was one of the surer things, as far as she was concerned. Grandma has been right so often that it is easy for me to think that she still is. So,

" 'Conrad's Sister's Shoulders,' Grandma."

ABOUT THE AUTHOR

CHANDLER W. STERLING IS A NATIVE OF Dixon, Illinois, a graduate of Northwestern University and received his Bachelor of Divinity Degree in 1938 and Doctor of Divinity in 1957 from Seabury-Western Theological Seminary. He has been rector of churches in Elmhurst, Illinois and Chadron, Nebraska and from 1956 to 1968 was Episcopal Bishop of Montana.

He is the author of five previous books, *The Arrogance of Piety*, *The Eighth Square*, *The Holyroyd Papers*, *Little Malice in Blunderland*, and *The Ice House Gang: My Year with the Black Hawks*. Bishop Sterling is now rector of Good Shepherd Church, Hilltown, Pennsylvania, where he lives with his family.